Fossil Digging
in Guilden and Steeple Morden

Bernard O'Connor

Few visitors to the quiet, rural settlements of Guilden and Steeple Morden, or even many of their residents, know of this area's role in the development of an industry of world importance. In the second part of the nineteenth century vast fortunes were made from the digging up, washing, transporting and processing of what were called "coprolites" thought at the time to be fossilised droppings of dinosaurs, fish and lizards! What follows is an examination of the social, religious and economic impact that this unusual industry had on the Mordents and surrounding parishes.

Many of Cambridge University Colleges, Cambridge surveyors and solicitors like Bidwell and Francis, local land-owning families and the clergy were very much involved in this unique and fascinating business. What follows is the story of this industry in the Mordens.

I have to acknowledge the research work done by David Short of Ashwell Field Studies Centre, Betty Wooton, Richard Grove, Walter Tye, Albert Sheldrick, Audrey Kiln and B. J. Davey. The Masters, Fellows, Students at Jesus College, Cambridge and St. John's College Cambridge very kindly provided me with access to their archives. I would also like to acknowledge the assistance of the staff at the following institutions: - Cambridgeshire and Hertfordshire County Record Offices, The Cambridge Collection, Cambridge University Library, Cambridge Folk Museum, Sedgwick Museum, Cambridge, The Public Record Office, Kew, The Valence House Museum, Dagenham, Church Commissioners' Record Office, London and the Charity Commissioners' Record Office, London.

Many others in the area have given snippets of information and encouragement but it is to the memory of those who worked in the diggings that this book is dedicated.

Similar accounts publications on the fossil diggings in other parishes can be found on: www.lulu.com/storefront/coprolite.
Read more of Bernard O'Connor's research on: www.bernardoconnor.org.uk

In 1856 a new industry started in the fields around Hinxworth, a small parish a few miles south of Guilden Morden. It provided a very different occupation to agricultural work, that of coprolite digging and locally called "fossiling." Until the nineteenth century the Mordens were small agricultural parishes that had not changed much since the Middle Ages. Over the first half of the century both parishes doubled in size. Guilden Morden's population increased 117% to 929 in 1851. Steeple Morden increased 106% over the same period to 888. Improved health care reduced the death rate and there was a strong tradition of large families in the 19th century. Ten children in the family was not uncommon. There were also strong feelings about social inequality which resulted in a high crime rate and significant out-migration. But beyond the rural communities of Cambridgeshire there were dramatic changes taking place.

The 18th and 19th century exodus from the countryside to the urban areas resulted in an enormous demand for accommodation and food. The ending of the Napoleonic Wars with the defeat of the French at Waterloo in 1815 brought a period of peace and prosperity to Britain. Its population doubled over the first half of the century. Towns and cities expanded rapidly on the coalfields and alongside the major rivers and canal system. People were attracted by the employment opportunities in industry, retail and commerce following the inventions of the Industrial Revolution. There were also many forced off the land by developments in the Agricultural revolution. The urban population needed feeding. The typical two-up two-down terraced houses didn't have the gardens to grow fruit or vegetables or space to keep a pig or chickens. People needed to buy food from the High Street, the market or the corner shops. Victorian entrepreneurs were quick to recognise the growing demand. Small family businesses dominated the business. As their profits grew they opened more shops, invested in better transport and had more money to buy from the farmers. If farmers could increase production there was more money to be made. Experiments began in an attempt to increase food production.

One can probably remember from one's schooldays Jethro Tull's seed drill, Lord 'Turnip' Townsend's four-course crop rotation method and the Earl of Norfolk and other agriculturalists' crossbreeding produced enormous pigs, cattle and sheep. But other experiments were going on with plants. The application of science and capital was being expended on agriculture as it had been on manufacturing. Once the chemists acknowledged that phosphate was a major nutrient in plant growth, the search was on to discover new supplies. In 1828 a rock phosphate, called phosphorite, started being exploited in Ontario, Canada. Chemists had found its value as a fertiliser and samples were tested in Great Britain. The German explorer, Humboldt, returned to Europe with details of the South American coastline and his report led to the European's "discovering" the use of "huano" or guano. This was an accumulation of tens of feet of phosphate-rich bird droppings that had impregnated discarded fish carcasses and bird skeletons on the Chincha Islands off the coast of Peru. The locals would not excavate it because of the smell so indentured Chinese labour was brought in. Shipping companies started to import it into Liverpool docks from 1838 where it was sold it at up to £12 per ton. This was much more expensive than bones but a successful advertising campaign in the agricultural press led to its widespread usage.

Other experiments included adding a whole range of materials to the soil. Blood, bones, soot, fish, seaweed, chalk, clay and even rags from discarded wool and cotton clothes were trialled. Maybe one can remember the rag and bone man? It was the waste product of the knife manufacturers in Sheffield, however, that sparked the interest in bones. It was found that the shavings from their knife handles proved a very effective fertiliser when added to the soil. (Voelcker, A. (1862), 'The International Exhibition at Paris,' p.149) The corn mills used by the agricultural suppliers were not able to meet the demand for bone meal and this led to the setting up of bone manure works. Their most popular products were half-inch bones. These were burnt or crushed and added to the soil as bone meal.

However, the bones from the knacker's yards were insufficient to meet the demand of the nation's manure manufacturers, a factor that led to the import of dried bones. There were reports of cargoes of mummified cats from Egyptian pyramids and sun-bleached bones from the North African desert and the Argentinean Pampas finding their way into the crushing mills. This was enough to prompt the comment by Baron Von Justus Liebig, that,

"*Great Britain is like a ghoul, searching the continents for bones to feed its agriculture ... robbing all other countries of the condition of her fertility. Already in her eagerness for bones she has turned up the battlefields of Leipzig, Waterloo, and of the Crimea; already from the catacombs of Sicily she has carried away the skeletons of many successive generations.*"

(Quoted in Keatley, W. S. (1976), '100 years of Fertiliser Manufacture,' Fertiliser Manufacturers Association; also in Pierre, W.H. and Norman, A.G. (Eds.) (1953), 'Soil Fertiliser Phosphorous in Crop Nutrition,' New York Academic Press, p. ix)

By 1839 the bone business was worth £150,000 per annum and about 30,000 tons were being imported annually. The Gardeners' Chronicle and Agricultural Gazette gave detailed accounts of the efficacy of these new manures. (Graham, J. (1839), 'A Treatise on the Use and Value of Manure', London p.6) However, tests showed that crushed bones were insoluble. It also took a long time before their mineral potential could be absorbed. Bones were also expensive and the machinery for grinding them had not been perfected. (Ibid.)

Life in the agricultural communities where these new ideas were being practised was not the quiet and peaceful rural idyll that characterised traditional images of country life. There were tremendous economic and social changes brought about in the nineteenth century. The introduction of the Enclosures after 1799 and the implementation of the new technology introduced during the "Agricultural Revolution" had a dramatic impact on rural villages. Many farm labourers became entirely dependent of the farmers for their livelihood. There were "hiring fairs" where men and women were taken on according to the decorations in their lapels. The historian, David Ellison, commented on the "startling" social effects that resulted.

"The repeal of the Corn Laws and the lower prices of corn for farmers had made them all try to save costs by mechanisation and reducing their labour forces... Cambridge's farm labourers had often noticed the immense gulf between themselves with their £25 to £30 a year, and the rectors with £300 - £400, comfortable rectories, and often land as well as house servants."

(Ellison, D. 'Coprolites in the Orwell area,' part of Orwell history topics; Ref. Latter Day Saints Millennial Star, passim, and Kowallis, Gay P. (1970?), 'To the Great Salt Lake from Litlington,' Bassingbourn)

Farm labourers were often provided with a tied cottage from which they could easily be evicted at the whim of the farmer or farm bailiff. Not being seen at church for the Sunday service was a dismissable offence. Going into the public house before the farmer and farm bailiff arrived after church was unwise. Crowds waited at the door in deference. There was considerable poverty and overcrowding in crumbling "shit and stubble" or wattle and daub thatched cottages in many rural villages. New steam-powered agricultural machinery, designed to save time and labour, was introduced by farmers who were keen to profit from the increased demand for food. These machines like the steam traction engine, threshing machine, deep plough and elevator resulted in an increasing number of redundancies in farm labour. Some people developed useful mechanical skills but there was widespread unrest in most rural communities. Many landless peasants were forced off the land when they lost the right to use the open fields. The loss of gleaning rights after harvest, the loss of the common for grazing animals and poultry, the denial of access to the newly fenced or walled in woodland reduced their "free" catch of rabbit, pheasant, partridge, nuts and wild fruit.

The more motivated sections of the community, mainly young adult males and females, left the countryside to find employment in the industrial towns and cities where better paid factory or domestic work was available. Some were attracted by the numerous advertisements in the Cambridge Chronicle and Royston Crow to emigrate. Hard working, temperate labourers and craftsmen were offered employment and land in the colonies in Canada, South Africa, Australia and New Zealand. Twenty-three villagers from Guilden Morden drowned on a voyage to Australia in 1845 that must have temporarily deterred others from leaving. (VCH., 'Cambs.' p.97; Holt. C. (1982), 'Assisted Emigration to Port Philip District, Victoria 1840 - 1870', paper in Ashwell Field Studies Centre) But it was another enterprise that halted this out-migration and very much brought this area into the Victorian era of industrial and economic change. Most of the villagers were engaged as agricultural labourers on the local farms and large estates or were employed as domestics in some of the country houses of the gentry. The Fordhams in Ashwell, for example, lived in larger properties with butlers, maids and gardeners whilst the villagers lived in small, cramped, thatched cottages with a small garden for growing fruit and vegetables, keeping a pig and chickens.

When the families got together at Easter and Christmas, for baptisms, marriages and funerals, stories of the changes in rural and urban life would have been common. With improvements in education and increases in the numbers of pamphlets, newspapers and journals there was a growing awareness of the disparity between town and countryside. For those who were unable to leave, some manifested their dissatisfaction with the state of affairs by acts of vandalism. This period, known as "The Swing", after the number of hangings of offenders, saw incidences of farm machinery being destroyed and haystacks, barns and even farmers' houses being set alight. (Fowle, K. (19--), 'Coton through the Ages') However, the discovery of a fossil seam reduced this unrest.

As shall be seen, this dissatisfaction diminished during the coprolite years with higher wages and a variety of new jobs available. What were these coprolites? "Coprolites," as they were called when they were first discovered, were thought to be fossilised droppings. There are numerous variations of their spelling, due in part to the poor literacy of the census enumerator but also to variations in local dialect. They include coprolite, copperlight, copper light, copperlite, coupperlite, copralite, corporolite, coprelite, coperlite, coporlite, coparlite, coprolithe and coperalite. No wonder there was confusion over their origin. (Analysis of the 1861 – 1891 census data) The word came from the Greek "kopros" meaning dung and "lithos" meaning stone. Dung stone - fossilised droppings! Rev. William Buckland, the Dean of Westminster, coined it when he was the first professor of Geology and Mineralogy at the University of Oxford. In 1829 he went on a geological excursion to the Dorset coast at Lyme Regis. Examining the clay and sands exposed by a recent landslip he found the complete fossil remains of an ichthyosaurus. Unusually, it also included its fossilised stomach contents.

Accompanying him on the excursion was the German analytical chemist, Baron Von Justus Liebig. He too was fascinated with the finds but the Dean was obsessed. He had a tabletop inlaid with polished coprolites as well as earrings made from polished slices! It is unknown if he wore them! His dinner parties were very entertaining. A bear used to wander around the dining room behind his guests and a monkey sat on furniture near the window. The menu often included samples from across the food chain, starting from plants and working through the animal kingdom! The worst tasting were reportedly moles and bluebottles! Dinnertime conversations included a challenge to the established religious circles. Buckland had found tiny bones of baby ichthyosaurus in the coprolites. This meant that ichthyosaurus ate ichthyosaurus. They were cannibals! This contradicted the fundamental religious belief that life before Adam was one of peace and harmony. Some argued that Adam and Eve frolicked with dinosaurs in Eden. Maybe the issue was discussed over dinner with Mr and Mrs Mantell who were the first to find Iguanodon remains in Sussex in 1822 and Sir Richard Owen who first came up with the word dinosaur to mean "terrible lizard". Owen was just as eccentric. On New Year's Eve 1853 he invited twenty scientists to a dinner party inside a life-size model of an iguanodon in a London park!

A similar discovery but one with far reaching implications was made in 1842. After Rev. John Henslow, the professor of Botany at St. John's College, Cambridge had been given a living by St. John's in the Suffolk parish of Hitcham, he went on a trip to the Victorian watering hole of Felixstowe. There had recently been a landslip in which he found some interesting fossils in the newly exposed Suffolk Crag at the bottom of the cliffs. There were loads of them. From their smooth, brown, elongated shape he took them to be fossilised dung, similar to those of the ichthyosaurus, discovered by Buckland. (O'Connor, B. (1998), 'Felixstowe's Fossil Industry', Bernard O'Connor, Gamlingay) He suspected that, like animal manure, they would be useful as a manure once they were ground to a powder. He was probably aware from reading about Suffolk's history that the Crag had been used on the fields for generations. In Walter Tye's research into the origins of the coprolite industry he noted that

"A Suffolk farmer first discovered the fertilizing value of the Suffolk red crag. I prefer that John Kirby, (Suffolk Traveller,1764) of Wickham Market, should tell the story in his own inimitable way :-

"In a Farmers Yard in Levington, clofe on the left as you enter from Levington into the faid Chapel Field of Stratton Hall, was dug the firft Crag of Shell that have been found ufeful for improving the land in this and other Hundreds in the neighbourhood. For though it appears from Books of Agriculture, that the like manure has long been ufeful in the Weft of England, it was not ufed here till this Difcovery was cafually made by one Edmund Edwards, about the year 1718. This man, being covering a Field with Muck out of his yard, and wanting a load of two to finifh it, carried fome of the Soil that laid near the Muck, tho' it looked to him no

better than Sand; but obferving the Crop to be beft where he laid that, he was from thence encouraged to carry more of it the next year; and the sucess he had, encouraged others to do the like." There is no need for me to explain that Edmund Edwards' discovery was soon broadcast throughout south-east Suffolk, where the crag was found. Large quantities were very soon carried and scattered over the heaths and sheep-walks, where the soil had always been hungry and inadequately fed."

(Walter Tye, 'Birth of Fertilizer Industry, 1930, Fisons Journal, p.4.)

Liebig had done some tests on Buckland's coprolites by dissolving them in vitriol, the term then used for sulphuric acid. His analysis of the resultant mass showed them to have a high phosphate content, a mineral much needed in plant growth. John Bennet Lawes, a Hertfordshire landowner, was experimenting with different manures on his estate in Rothamsted. Like Liebig, he too successfully dissolved animal bones, the mineral phosphorite and Felixstowe coprolites in vitriol. The resulting mixture, once dried and bagged, he called "super phosphate of lime". His tests showed that it was soluble in water and that the plant roots could rapidly absorb it. He experiments with it on plants in pots and test beds showed it to be extremely valuable manure, especially for root crops. His "super" was the world's first artificial chemical manure and its application so dramatically increased turnip yields that it became much in demand by the nation's farmers. They were eager to improve supplies of winter fodder. This was because once the harvest was in and farmers knew how much fodder was available over winter, large numbers of surplus cattle, sheep or pigs had to be slaughtered. Meat commanded higher prices over winter until the new stock was brought onto the market in spring. Any way of providing increased fodder therefore would be very popular with farmers.

Much to Lawes' pleasure the results of his tests with his new manure showed that it was effective on a whole range of other crops. He patented his "discovery" in 1842, which annoyed Liebig who claimed to have been the first to do it. It also upset Lawes' mother who was appalled that a gentleman should engage in trade - let alone in manure. Ignoring both he set up his own company. It was called "Lawes Artificial Manure Company." His fiancée could not have been pleased. The planned European Tour for their honeymoon was cancelled in favour of a trip down the Thames during which he spotted an ideal site for his factory. He bought a plot at Deptford and had a large chemical manure works built that was capable of producing up to 200 tons of superphosphate a week. He sold his "super" at up to £7.00 a ton and took legal action against Liebig and others to ensure that anyone who wanted to use his patent had to pay him five shillings (£0.25) for every ton they produced. (Dyke, G.V. (1993), 'John Lawes of Rothamsted' Hoos Press, Harpenden, p.15)

Maybe Henslow was in correspondence with Lawes as he realised that the Felixstowe fossil bed could be a valuable source of manure. As a wide range of animal manure was being put onto the fields he thought that fossilised droppings could be used for the same purpose. In 1845 he read a paper in Cambridge to the British Association for the Advancement of Science. (Henslow, Rev. John, (1845), Report to British Association, Cambridge) It dealt with their potential value to the nation's farmers. Suffolk manure manufacturers like William Colchester, Edward Packard and Joseph Fison took interest. They made arrangements with Felixstowe landowners to have the fossils dug up, washed and transported to their works in Ipswich. A few shillings a ton royalty was offered for the fossils. As a cheap alternative to the other manures on the market, there was keen interest in coprolites.

Maybe it was the reports of Rev. Henslow's speech that prompted a local farmer to show him some fossils that he had dug up on his property. Charles Kingsley, one of Henslow's students, must have been present as he recorded Henslow's response.

"He saw, being somewhat of, a geologist and chemist, that they were not, as fossils usually are, carbonate of lime, but phosphate of lime - bone earth. He said at once, as by inspiration, "You have found a treasure - not a gold-mine, indeed, but a food-mine. This bone earth, which we are at our wit's end to get for our grain and pulses; which we are importing, as expensive bones, all the way from Buenos Ayres. Only find enough of them, and you will increase immensely the food supply of England and perhaps make her independent of foreign phosphates in case of war."

(Anonymous note in Ipswich Museum's Coprolite file)

A treasure? A food-mine? Such a response must have astounded the farmer. It is undocumented where the farmer was from but it is thought that he was from Burwell, a fenland parish north of Cambridge. Fossils had been found beneath the fenland peat from as early as 1816. (Hailstone, Rev. J. (1816), 'Outlines of the Geology of Cambridgeshire', Phil. Trans. Royal. Soc., pp.243-250) Their discovery was related to an important fenland occupation, locally called "claying". This involved the digging of small pits through the "moor" or "bear's muck", as the bog-earth was called, to reach the clay. This lay between two and ten feet (0.74m. - 3.7m.) below the surface. Wearing waterproofed boots the diggers would use a sharp, cutting-edged shovel to dig through the peat, a light wooden scoop to get rid of drainage water and an axe or "bill" to excavate the clay beneath. The top metre of clay was thrown to the sides of the pit and then mixed into the peat.

The material turned up by this "claying" occasionally included fossils of what were thought to be bears and oxen. When Burwell Fen started to be drained in the early-1800s the excavation of drainage ditches or "lodes" exposed an extensive bed of fossils. A local farmer, John Ball, noticed that the turnips he grew on the clayey, fossil deposit that had been mixed into his peat soil produced dramatically better yields than the crops on fields he had not clayed. The Burwell doctor, Mr Lucas, explained that the "extraordinary liveliness" was related to the high phosphate content of the fossils. ('The Farming of Cambridgeshire,' Royal Agric.Soc.1847, p.71; Lucas, C. (1930), 'The Fenman's World - Memories of a Fenland Physician,' (Norwich), p.25)

Dr. Lucas may well have heard about Rev. Henslow's Cambridge speech or read about it in the local press. Aware of the potential demand by manure manufacturers and maybe even knowing the farmer who had shown Henslow the fossils, he suspected that the Burwell deposit could also be a matter of "commercial proposition". Their shallow depth beneath the fenland peat just above the gault clay would allow them to be raised without very high labour costs. The proximity of Burwell Lode allowed easy access by barge or lighter to Popes Corner - the confluence of the Ouse and the Cam - and then via Ely, Littleport and Downham Market onto King's Lynn and then transhipped to Ipswich or London.

With an eye for speculation and without having first seen it, he bought some eleven acres of Burwell Fen. The locals thought he had taken leave of his senses. A month later, so the story goes, he went by boat up Burwell Lode with "an interested party" to locate the deposit. After rowing for some time, they reached a point about a mile west of the village where the potential buyer was handed a "sprit" and told to push it into the land below the boat. (Gathercole, A. F. (1959), 'Fenland Village,' Fisons Journal, No.64 Sept. pp.24-9; Suffolk County Record Office (SCRO) HC 438.8728/269)

The depth of the seam was not noted but the locals were astounded when he sold the plot and the coprolites beneath it for £1,000. Realising almost £100 per acre was a phenomenal profit, given that agricultural rents ranged at that time from about ten to forty shillings (£0.50 - £2.00) an acre. The "interested party" was William Colchester, one of the Suffolk manure manufacturers who also had investments in brick manufacturing and ships. In 1846 he expanded his manure business by building a new manure works in Ipswich. According to a later geological paper he had raised 500 tons by 1847.

(Lucas, C. (1930), op.cit; Reid, C. (1890), 'Nodule Bed,' Memoirs of the Geological Survey (MGS) p.16)

Others speculated in the new industry. Edward Packard, a chemist from Saxmundham in Suffolk successfully processed the Felixstowe "coprolites" and in 1847 he opened his own manure factory on the banks of the River Orwell in Ipswich. Joseph Fison, part of a milling and baking family, had moved into Ipswich in 1840. He established a factory at Stoke Bridge and converted it to process coprolites and other phosphatic material in 1850. (Fisons Journal, No.77, December 1963; Norsk Hydro file, Museum of East Anglian Life, Stowmarket)

Lawes, Colchester, Packard and Fison advertised their superphosphate in the pages of the "Gardeners Chronicle and Agricultural Gazette" and the "Mark Lane Express" thus realising Henslow's idea. Articles on its successful application and of using coprolites in its manufacture appeared in the agricultural press. These increased landowners and agriculturalists' awareness of the financial advantages of locating the fossil deposit on their properties.

So, by the 1850s, Rev. Buckland realised that his discovery had led to the birth of a new industry exploiting fossil beds in Suffolk and Cambridgeshire. He questioned the possibility that these

> "...excretions of extinct animals contained the mineral ingredients of so much value in animal manure. The question was in fact not yet solved by the chemist, and we took specimens, in order to confirm by chemical analysis the views of the geologist. After Liebig had completed their analysis, he saw that they might be made applicable to practical purposes.
> What a curious and interesting subject for contemplation! In the remains of an extinct animal world England is to find the means of increasing her wealth in agricultural produce, as she has already found the great support of her manufacturing industry in fossil fuel - the

preserved matter of primeval forests - the remains of a vegetable world! May this expectation be realised! and may her excellent population be thus redeemed from poverty and misery!

I well recollect the storm of ridicule raised by these expressions of the German philosopher, and yet truth has triumphed over scepticism, and thousands of tons of similar animal remains are now used in promoting the fertility of our fields. The geological observer, in his search after evidences of ancient life, aided by the chemist, excavated extinct remains which produced new life to future generations."

(Anonymous author, 'The Study of Abstract Science Essential to the Progress of Industry,' Memoirs of Geological Survey, Mineral Statistics, vol. i, 1850?, pp.40-1)

Many people thought that the fossils were the droppings of bear, lizard or fish or even dinosaur droppings. A retired major from Reach thought that they resembled sun-dried wildebeest droppings. They were similar to those he had seen on the flood plains of the Zambezi once the vast herds had passed. Students and professors at Cambridge University's newly established Geology department became very interested in the range of fossils being thrown up. There was extensive debate in geological circles and many argued that the deposit ought not to be termed coprolite. They should more correctly be termed pseudo-coprolites or phosphatic nodules. However, the trade name "coprolites" stuck. Recently however, an excellent example of some poor creature's rectal content has been found in Barrington that gives credence to the locals' views. One can make out the pressure creases and a sharp point as if it was its last squeeze. Photographs of this and typical Cambridgeshire coprolites can be seen in the illustrations.

The bulk of the deposit was of misshapen, black/grey lumps but amongst them were found the teeth, bones, scales and claws of Jurassic and Cretaceous dinosaurs. They included craterosaurus, dakosaurus, dinotosaurus, megalosaurus, iguanodon and the pterodactyl. Prehistoric marine reptiles of ichthyosaurus, plesiosaurus and pliosaurus were found as well as the remains of whale, shark, turtle and a huge variety of shells, sponges and other marine organisms. The most common was the ammonite. Other animals that were discovered in the diggings included crocodiles, hippopotamus, elephant, rhinoceros, lion, hyena, tapir, bear, horse and oxen - evidence of this area's tropical past. (O'Connor, B. (1998), 'The Dinosaurs on Sandy Heath', Bernard O'Connor, Gamlingay) There were also lumps of what some argue are inorganic calcium phosphate. But why is it that such a variety of creatures that you would normally expect to see in hot tropical countries in Africa were found in Cambridgeshire?

When the European plate broke away from Pangaea about 500 million years ago it was south of the Equator. It was during this period that the gault clay was deposited. This area was about 28° S, where Namibia is today! To reach its present latitude this area has moved over 80° of the planet's surface, thousands of miles. It experienced a range of differing environments on its slow movement north from the tropical and equatorial forests, swamps, savannah grassland and desert to today's temperate latitudes about 55° N. But what had produced such an enormous prehistoric graveyard? A number of the Victorian geologists considered that the Jurassic and Cretaceous fossil deposits had been washed out of the clays which were exposed when the south of England was uplifted from the sea to produce the Weald. A recent theory is that about 94 million years ago sea levels rose dramatically, flooding the London-Brabant Basin, of which present day Cambridgeshire formed its northern coast. This wiped out much of the animal population. Carbon dioxide given off by the flood basalts released by the tectonic activity also played their part. Many of the land creatures would have been poisoned and also the marine life that had to come up to the surface for air. Some suggested that as the bodies accumulated as debris in coastal embayments their bones, teeth, scales and claws gradually absorbed the phosphoric acid from overlying deposits of decaying organisms. Another theory was that the calcium absorbed dissolved phosphate from the seawater. It was said that the rivers had dissolved the apatite, a phosphatic mineral found in the volcanic rocks of Scandinavia and Scotland, which impregnated the deposit and explains their higher phosphate content than today's animal and human bones.

Analysis of amber samples shows that at the time when dinosaurs were at their greatest size, about 230 million years ago, the oxygen content of the air was 35%. Over the Cretaceous period it gradually declined as a result of the increased carbon dioxide released into the atmosphere by extensive volcanic activity. Levels fell to 11% 65 million years ago and today they are 21%. Dinosaurs had to adapt to these changing conditions. It was like having asthma, not getting enough oxygen into the blood. They had to build enough energy to catch prey - the "dash and dine" characteristic of today's crocodiles. Many were exhausted, maybe too tired for sex even. Like crocodiles they buried their eggs. It is thought that increased temperatures meant that they had single-sex populations that further reduced numbers. The leathery skin of their eggs absorbed the poisonous gases and embryos failed to develop. In order to survive these changing conditions dinosaurs had to evolve with a much-reduced size. A cataclysmic catastrophe like a rise in sea level of hundreds of feet as well as poisoned air could explain the huge numbers of creatures found in the East Anglian fossil beds. Given the volume of the creatures, they must have piled up on each other into a layer many tens of feet thick in hollows on the seabed. The upper bodies would have been eaten by any of the surviving marine life like ammonites and worms but the lower bodies, without oxygen for decomposition, gradually fossilised as the upper layers were covered in the hundreds of feet of Cambridgeshire Greensand. This was probably washed into the ocean from the arid parts of the continent still above sea level.

Compressed by this strata and the subsequent chalk marl of Eastern and Southern Cambridgeshire they gradually fossilised.

This could explain why there are real coprolites in the deposit. The contents of stomachs, intestines and rectums would have been found along with bones, teeth, claws, scales and shells. Throughout the deposit were found large numbers of ammonites, squid-like creatures that scavenged on the sea floor but there were oyster shells on the upper surface. Over the millions of years, fluctuations in sea level exposed the soft Greensand and differential erosion uncovered the fossils at its base. The remains would have been washed around, so that one does not find whole skeletons in the deposit. Many of the surface features of the remains were removed by abrasion but lines showing worm tracks are often visible along the nodules, the biggest of which rarely extend over six inches (15cms).

Further inundation resulted in a second bed accumulating which was covered once more with Greensand deposits and then hundreds of feet of chalk. This latter deposit was made up from minute marine organisms whose bodies contained calcium carbonate. When sea levels eventually fell these more recent deposits were exposed the to the elements. The upper layers would have been eroded and the chalk and sand gradually lowered to expose the fossil beds. The sixteen ice ages contributed most to the erosion removing hundreds of feet of rock to leave the low chalk and sandy ridges of East Anglia.

Whilst the bed was one of great fascination to the country's geologists, its commercial value was not in how much they could be sold to those Victorians fascinated by fossils. Another of Rev. Henslow's students at Cambridge was Charles Darwin. His evolutionary theories caused a storm when they were published in 1858 and further stimulated the enormous interest in geology, palaeontology, anthropology and archaeology. Many Victorian drawing rooms had specimens from the Greensand displayed in glass-sided cabinets. They were also eagerly bought up by geology students and their professors as well as by museum curators across the country. Perhaps the best specimens can be found in the Sedgwick Earth Sciences Museum in Cambridge.

Their main value, however, was as a raw material for manure manufacturers. And not just in this country but also overseas. In the late-1840s landowners were offered as little as a few shillings a ton for the coprolites. As more and more businesses joined in the rush for manures demand for coprolite rose. Royalties they paid landowners rose to between seven and fifteen shillings a ton in the early 1850s. They depended on a range of factors. The depth, extent, continuity of the seam, the angle of dip, its cleanliness, the nearness to a water source, road, wharf or station, the volume coming onto the market, knowledge or ignorance of current prices and, inevitably, nepotism - how well the contractor knew the landowner.

A new extractive industry began - an alternative and much more profitable line of work than digging clunch, clay or turf. When the fossil seam was noticed in the Chesterton brick fields in 1848 the owners sold some of what they considered "troublesome annoyances" to Mr Deck, a chemist of Fitzroy Street, Cambridge for £2 per ton. He probably was not told the royalties the Suffolk manure manufacturers were paying but would have known that similar "phosphatic nodules" were being raised in the Felixstowe and Burwell areas. The tests he did on them showed that the Cambridgeshire "coprolites" had between 50% - 60% calcium phosphate, up to 10% higher than the Suffolk variety. It stimulated their extraction as *"a matter of commercial proposition."* (Cambridge Independent Press (CIP), 18th January, p.3)

When it was found that the seam extended to the south under Coldham's Common in Barnwell, the industry took off on a large scale. Some Suffolk manure manufacturers and entrepreneurial coprolite contractors, keen to capitalise on the demand, moved into the area to win agreements with brickyard and other landowners to raise the fossils. Gangs of experienced diggers came over to run the Cambridgeshire pits from Suffolk and other counties. (O'Connor, B. (1998), 'The Dinosaurs on Coldham's Common', Bernard O'Connor, Gamlingay) This in-migration was not evidenced directly in the 1851 census however. There was no reference to fossil or coprolite diggers, coprolite contractors or merchants in any of the parishes where it was then being worked. It is thought that the work was just considered as labouring or, if they were employed by a farmer, as agricultural labour. Guilden Morden's population had increased 14% over the 1840s to 929 and Steeple Morden's increased 11% to 888. How many had left the area has not been determined.

It was hardly a coincidence that the geological mapping of the country started around this time. Whilst the exploration was mainly for scientific reasons, knowledge of the extent and distribution of the Greensand was of commercial importance to those who had money to invest in what was to become known as the coprolite diggings.

The seam averaged about thirty inches (about 39cm.) thick but in places was up to six feet (2.1 metres). In some areas it was non-existent, locally called "dead land," due to a slight rise in the seabed whilst the fossils had tended to accumulate in the hollows. Yields therefore varied. In Cambridge itself it was about 300 tons per acre (0.404ha.). In one pit in Wicken it was 2,000 tons but the average was 250 tons per acre. (Kingston, A. (1889) 'Old and New Industries on the Cam.' Warren Press, Royston p.16) When annual agricultural rents were rarely over fifty shillings (£2.50) an acre and these coprolites could be sold at over £2.00 per ton, potentially several hundred pounds could be realised from an acre! Wages of agricultural labourers at that time wouldn't have been over £25 in a year and £200 could have bought a small estate. No wonder there was a lot of interest in them. So began what has been termed by the historian, Richard Grove, as "The Cambridgeshire Coprolite Mining Rush." (Oleander Press, Cambridge, 1976)

The depth and extent of the bed had to be determined. This was done initially by digging a coffin-like pit. A cheaper method was by using a two-man corkscrew borer. Walter Tye, in his account of the Suffolk industry included an interview with one of the diggers who said that

"To test the depth of the coprolite he made use of a tool like a giant corkscrew, called a 'dipper,' which shuddered in his hands when striking the mineral. Local cottagers always knew what the foreman was after when he came into their gardens carrying his 'dipper.' Naturally, they strongly objected to their gardens being turned topsy-turvy, however much coprolite he might find there, and they were always delighted to see him go. Old residents today say that a sixpenny tip usually had the desired effect."

(Tye, W. op.cit. p.8.)

In places the deposit was found outcropping on the surface but in most cases it had to be dug from between ten and twenty feet (3.7 – 7.4m.) of chalk marl. Where it was found on a small property it was simple matter for the landowner to take on a gang of labourers and have the fossils dug up, washed and sorted and then carted off and sold to a manure manufacturer. In this case it was commonly the farmer's own agricultural labourers. They used to dig the fossils during the low season, once the harvest was in. The work continued over the winter months and then the pits would be left to allow the farm work to start in spring.

If the land was copyhold then the tenant might get permission to raise it using their labourers but occasionally, where a large-scale operation was envisaged, they were evicted and a coprolite manager allowed to move in to the farmhouse. On larger properties an advertisement might be placed in the local press and tenders invited for a contractor to do the work. This occasionally led to existing tenants being given notice to quit to allow the coprolite manager a house to live in whilst the works were in operation but, more often than not, they were compensated for the loss of revenue from those fields which were being dug. Farmers and others set themselves up as coprolite contractors and took on a gang of men and boys. Pick axes, crowbars, shovels, planks, dog irons (supports for the planks), wheelbarrows, trucks and tramway had to be bought and a horse or steam-operated washmill had to be erected to clean the soil and clay from the fossils. A tool shed was erected and another for sorting, having lunch or sheltering from the rain. All this cost money and local bank managers were keen to make loans to enterprising individuals in an industry that had such high returns.

Women and girls were employed in large numbers where the deposit was found in sandier areas. Here the fossils needed sorting to remove any unwanted stones that would reduce the quality and therefore the price paid by the manure manufacturers. There is no evidence of any female employment in the Mordens area. The main female employment was in Wicken in the fens and Potton, near Sandy in Bedfordshire.

Contractors agreed to do the work over a set number of years with them paying the landowner a royalty of so much per ton. The tenant farmer was often compensated for the loss of revenue from those fields out of cultivation by up to £10 an acre. Once work got started the topsoil and subsoil was barrowed to one side of the field to be replaced later. In many cases it was used as the base of the washmill. As the coprolite seam was exposed the diggers shovelled it into wheelbarrows or emptied it into trucks. These were then pushed by hand or pulled by horses along a tramway that ran out of the pit, along the edge of the field or trackway to the washmill. Here their contents were unloaded to create large piles before they were washed and sorted. The soil above the seam on the new face was removed after undercutting, a process which caused considerable danger. Crowbars, pick-axes and shovels were used to make it collapse and, for convenience, it was just thrown into the trench already worked. As shall be seen there were numerous cases of accidents in the pits caused by collapses. This "backfilling" meant that the labourers gradually progressed across the field and onto adjoining property where a new lease was sought. Sometimes pits were opened at opposite ends of the field and two gangs of diggers gradually dug their way towards each other.

The job of washing the fossils got progressively easier over the years. Initially the technique in Suffolk was to dig a trench into the side of the estuary or the river. The actual washing and screening process was described in Walter Tye's fascinating insights into the diggings.

> *"That was an old man's job when he became too old for the pit. A long tank some thirty feet in length, was specially provided for the job. The coprolites, along with a certain amount of dirt and bones, were shovelled into sieves which, when full, were placed on a ledge in the tank, just under the surface of the water; to each sieve was fastened a long pole, which the washer pulled backwards and forwards until the stones were clean. When there was a shortage of water, in or near the pit, the washing was done at the quayside before loading."*

(Tye, W. op.cit. pp.3-10)

In Cambridgeshire, without access to a tidal estuary, innovative engineers used their skills to develop sophisticated washmills powered by horse or steam engine. A mound was constructed using the top and subsoil. On top of this mound a circular brick base was laid onto which a circular iron tray was placed. Large sections of the iron plates that formed the base of one such washmill have been found on Rectory Farm, Whaddon. Barrowloads of fossils were wheeled up the mound and emptied into the tray. A pump was often installed to bring the huge quantities of water needed from a nearby water source. Wells sometimes had to be dug and lined with bricks. At one time there were eleven such mills in operation in the Bassingbourn area which were claimed to have been responsible for lowing the water table of the area. (Whitaker, W. (1921), 'Water Supply of Cambs.' MGS, London, p.84. There is a photograph of a circular coprolite harrow in Cambridgeshire Collection W27.1. KO. 19554)

The working of these mills was described by the son of the Burwell doctor, Mr Lucas, whose coprolite land was the first to be exploited in Cambridgeshire-. Once the coprolite had been brought to the surface: -

> "The first thing to do was to throw up a hill in the middle of the ground, and this was done by first erecting- a post about ten or twelve feet long, and throwing the soil around it to a height of eleven or twelve feet and of thirty feet in diameter. Three feet from the centre a ring would be formed six to eight feet wide and four feet deep. This would be paved with bricks and the sides would be sheets of iron. On one side of the hill a platform was made from a wooden tank, to which was connected a pump eighteen feet long; a pipe from the tank would go with the ring and opposite the tank was a trapped outlet, and on the outer side of the hill a square of about two chains would be earthed up a little to form a sort of pan. From the central post a wooden arm would be attached about twelve to fourteen feet long; to this would be attached a wimpole tree, to which a horse would be yoked. Connected to the centre of the post would be a light rail which was fixed to the horse bridle to keep the horse always in is track; from the arm would be suspended two iron harrows which ran well in on the bottom of the ring. When the soil containing the fossils was wheeled up to the ring a sufficient quantity of water would be let in. As the horse went round a creamy fluid would be produced and the fossils would drop on the floor. Then the trapped outlet would be opened and the creamlike fluid, called "slurry" would flow into pans. This operation having been repeated a number of times the fossils on the floor would be washed clear of earth and weighed up".

(Lucas, C. (1931), 'The Fenman's World', Norwich, p.31)

The cost of constructing these mills in the late-1840s when they were first developed was £100 but by 1875 the "coprolite contractors had become so expeditious that a hill could be put up *for £5!* (Ibid.) A description of such mills was recorded in a tourist's account of a trip in the fens.

"As we return from Burwell our eyes rest on several raised circular enclosures, round which a number of often grey horses are almost ceaselessly walking. These are the mills erected for washing the fossils. These fossils or coprolites are valuable on account of the calcic phosphate contained in them."

(Eade, David, (18--), 'Rambles in Cambridgeshire', Soham, p.48)

As the technology improved, steam powered washmills were introduced by those contractors who could afford it. After several such washings the dirty water, locally termed "slub" or "slurry" was run back into "slurry pans" to dry out before the topsoil was replaced. The theory was that once dried the cracks in it would allow better drainage. As the work progressed across the field the mill was transferred to a more accessible site. The topsoil was barrowed back into the trench or slurry pit and levelled ready for cultivation. Whilst the theory was that this process would improve the soil, in practise the operation was not always done thoroughly. It was cheaper for a contractor to cover it up quickly and move on. A farmer, however, would take care as he would benefit from improved cropping. In several areas white chalk markings can still be seen on the fields which indicate where slurry was not properly covered or the topsoil replaced. Astute land agents ensured that agreements included very precise instructions for this process and subsequent drainage, levelling and seeding.

Horses would have been a common sight hauling tumbrils loaded with washed coprolites along the Road to Odsey station on the Bedford to Cambridge branch of the Great Eastern Railway. From here railway trucks would take them to manure factories in Ipswich, London and elsewhere. Some would have been taken into Cambridge to the wharf by Silver Street bridge. A barge or fenland lighter would take them up the Cam and Ouse to King's Lynn for transhipment round the coast. Others were carted direct to local bone mills like Walton's on East Road, Cambridge or the Cambridge Manure Company's works on Histon Road. This company was set up in the early-1850s by the Cambridge auctioneer, John Rolfe Mann, a Fulbourn merchant, A. P. Chaplin, and other "agriculturalists" and entrepreneurs who recognised the profits to be made in this lucrative business. The Cambridge solicitor, Clement Francis, was to act as their "undisclosed agent." (Cambridge Collection, Cooper's Misc. Papers, 32. 1856; Cambridgeshire County Record Office (CCRO), Francis & Co. Bill Books, 1855 pp.455,539; CCRO R60/3 Cambridge Manure Co. Minute Books.) Many local bone and corn mills had to be converted as the gritstone was not hard enough to grind the coprolites. A hard buhrstone had to be installed in its place.

With "super" being sold at up to £7 a ton, half the price of guano, it became much in demand across the country. It was not long therefore before sales were being promoted across Europe, in America and throughout the Empire. There were reports of sales as far afield as Russia and Queensland. (O'Connor, B. (1998) 'The Dinosaurs on Coldham's Common', Bernard O'Connor, Gamlingay) During the 1850s there were four manure factories in Cambridge. With them paying an average forty-three shillings and sixpence (£2.18) a ton in 1856 for Cambridge coprolites there were profits to be made by coprolite contractors and merchants. By the 1870s the deposit was mapped in most of the Eastern Counties. Although the Upper and Lower Greensand beds were not continuous, the fossils at their base were worked in parts of Suffolk, Norfolk, Cambridgeshire, Hertfordshire, Bedfordshire, Buckinghamshire, Oxfordshire, Hampshire, Yorkshire and Kent. Its enormous extent allowed many new manure companies to capitalise on this new raw material and take a share of the increasing market for artificial fertilisers. Accordingly, many new chemical manure works were opened on the coprolite belt in

Burwell, Duxford, Shepreth, Royston, Bassingbourn and Odsey. The extent of the coprolite belt across this area can be seen in the illustrations.

James Ind Headley, the Cambridge iron founder who built the famous Eagle steam engine, was very much involved in the coprolite business. He had his own coprolite works erected behind his Eagle Foundry on Mill Road in Cambridge and had his works, "*well fitted up to make the pumps, washmills, cast iron screens and steam engines to provide power.*" (Enid Porter's notebooks Cambridge Folk Museum 15/64-65) He was aware of the investment opportunities in this area and luck had it that one of his relatives lived in Coton whose land was dug for coprolites. In the early-1850s coprolite contractors were paying landowners royalties of between seven and fifteen shillings a ton for all the coprolites they raised. This entailed having a weighbridge set up by the works and for accurate measurements to be recorded. To avoid errors and dependence on the contractors' weighings the land agents suggested an alternative scheme whereby royalties should be paid according to how many acres were dug over the year. This entailed having the pits surveyed around Lady Day (May 1st) and Michaelmas (September 29th) The surveyor's measurements could then be used to determine how much the contractor owed. This provided local companies like Bidwell, Francis, Smith, Carter Jonas and Mann and Raven a valuable additional source of income for the next forty years. Royalties ranged from as high as £400 to as low as £30 an acre but the average was about £100. This was about forty to fifty times the revenue the landowners could get from agricultural rents. After labour and other costs were deducted the contractors could make a big profit.

Throughout the 1850s the seam was worked in Cambridge and some nearby parishes. With the development of mass-production in the brick and tile making industry, landowners were able to bring a lot more clay land under cultivation. This was done by laying down drainage tiles. The trenching work for this, or deep ploughing, often revealed the seam a few feet below the surface. By 1856 the seam had been discovered along the foot of Coton Ridge, just west of Cambridge. Work started at the same time in fields east of Barton, in Little Eversden and Orwell where it was found around the edges of several low hills of chalk marl that overlay the gault clay. (Kelly's Post Office Directory, Orwell, 1864) In his historical account of the parish the vicar, Rev. A.C. Yorke, and nephew of Charles Phillip Yorke, the 5th Earl of Hardwicke, stated that the coprolite digging, *"somewhere about 1856 forced its way onto the Wimpole estates."* (Cambridge University Library, (CUL.) Palmer Papers B51, Yorke, A.C. (1979), 'Wimpole as I knew it,' p.12)

It was also that year when they started in Hinxworth. Rev. Robert Clutterbuck had arranged the drainage of his estate which uncovered the seam. In his 1877 account of the coprolite beds he described his holding at that time.

"The estate lies at the bottom of the Chalk escarpment of the London basin, and covers a portion of the lowest bed of the Chalk, the outcrop of the Greensand, and a portion of the gault of the Greensand formation. In several parts a superficial drifted gravel and sand overlies the older beds. The Greensand separating the Chalk from the gault is very thin, and, if collected in a distinct layer, would not exceed three inches in its thickest part...

"In the years 1856-8 Mr B. Denton carried out some drainage works for me in the parish of Hinxworth, over an area of 800 acres... I necessarily became aware of the existence on my own property of the seam which contains the coprolite bed. The discovery by Liebig of dissolving bones in sulphuric acid for the purpose of manure had at that time given a commercial value to these phosphatic nodules and they were eagerly sought for by the manufacturers of mineral phosphates for agricultural purposes. "

(Clutterbuck, Robert, (1877), 'The Coprolite Beds at Hinxworth,' Trans. Watford Natural History Soc. Vol. 1. p.238)

The fact that mass-produced clay pipes were now available more cheaply and in greater quantities enabled Rev. Clutterbuck to bring his newly enclosed Gault land into cultivation. His surveyor and engineer was John Bailey Denton of London. He would probably have read in the agricultural press that these fossil bones were being exploited on a large scale in Suffolk as well as in Cambridge and neighbouring parishes. The business was also bringing in considerable fortunes to all those involved. In order to exploit their economic potential he went into business with a London merchant, Edward Dicey. (Victoria County History, 'Hertfordshire', vol.iii,1912,p.232) On the 28th of October, 1856, they were granted a licence,

"...to dig work quarry and search for a certain mineral or fossil substance called or known by the name of coprolites in the parish of Hinxworth (Middle Farm and Hinxworth Place) in respective occupations of Richard Sale and Edward Sale and to occupy a piece of land (30 on Estate Plan) Hill Field and to dig work and quarry the coprolites there found to raise and bring to the surface and then to wash dress grind crush and make merchantable and fit for sale and the same to take carry away convert and dispose of for their own use... and to dig work and make such Adits pits trenches tramways winzes drifts cuts and watercourses and to erect such sheds buildings and machinery and also to sink such wells and construct such roads John Bailey Denton and Edward Dicey consider necessary or convenient for the effectual exercise of the liberty [this] licence powers..,.

(Hertfordshire County Record Office (HCRO), 28250)

The licence entitled them to a period of twenty-one years with an arrangement to pay Rev. Clutterbuck £20 for each excavation and that every quarter they should pay him one eighth of the coprolite's sale price. There was a stipulation that it should be no less than five shillings (£0.25) a ton. Given that manure manufacturers paid on average £2.10 per ton, it was a profitable investment. (CCRO. R60/3 Cambridge Manure Co. Minute books 1857-1860) Another important clause in their agreement was that they had to agree

> "...to deposit, restore and replace all surface and upper soil and so level and fill up all the trenches, wells and cavities to be made in a proper and workmanlike manner as to produce the least possible resulting or permanent injury to the surface of the ground."
>
> (HCRO. 28250)

There was no indication that Messrs Sale were to be compensated for the loss of use of their fields, only compensated for any crop or tillage damage. The licence actually granted Dicey and Denton almost 500 acres, an enormous area, 247a.3r.35p. on Middle Farm and 222a.2r.36p. on Hinxworth Place Farm. (Enclosure Map field numbers 4, 5, 17-24, 27-29, 38-45, 48 on Middle Farm and Fields 58-76, 30 on Hinxworth Place)

They formed "Messrs. Dicey and Denton" company and set up a large-scale operation with washmills, wells and tramways. This was the first recorded operation of its kind in Hertfordshire and accordingly attracted the attention of the Hertfordshire Guardian. It reported in May 1857 on a group of visitors being taken round the area to observe the advantages of a newly drained estate.

> "Crossing the road eastward, the company passed through a field, and then came to a place where a very interesting process was going on - the washing of coprolites. These coprolites, it is generally, and with good reason, believed, are the fossilised dung of extinct animals; and, containing a large percentage of phosphate of lime, are valuable for manures. Mr Denton found them lying on the gault in the green sand, and, paying a small royalty per ton, he washes them free of sand and clay by means of a circular trough, into which water passes. A roller of iron spikes stirs up the sand by means of horsepower, and this passes off below, leaving the coprolites at the bottom. Some curious relics of the antediluvian, or probably of the pre-Adamite,

world are to be found among the coprolites. We picked up several shark's teeth, belemnites, spines of aconites, fossilised oysters, bones &c; and the workmen engaged have found still more valuable remains of former ages. The coprolites are worth 38s per ton on the spot, or 40s at the rail, and we hope Mr Denton will be repaid for his enterprise. He raises about 250 tons per acre."

(Herts. Guardian,12th May 1857)

Potentially it was a very lucrative business with up to £500 being realised from every acre before royalties, plant and labour costs. Because one eighth of the sale price was less than five shillings (£0.25) Clutterbuck would have received about £60 per acre. This would have been more when the prices manure manufacturers paid for the coprolites increased. Transport costs of two shillings (£0.10) per ton must have proved a welcome source of income for local carters. Their horses hauled truckloads of the washed coprolites on a tramway along the "Ridgeway" to the main road in Ashwell and then on to Odsey Mill. This was erected in 1846 by Herbert Fordham who converted it shortly afterwards to grind the coprolites. Grinding added value to the coprolites and, cheaper than "super", ground coprolite was purchased by those farmers who wanted to make the fertiliser themselves. This was evidenced when Dicey and Denton's partnership was dissolved in 1858. The reason for the break-up was not stated but the documents related to the subsequent arrangements stated that they had been involved in "manufacturing coprolites and manure made thereof at Hinxworth and Ashwell and vending the same." (HCRO. 28252) There was no indication of any disagreement between them but with Denton busy with the Ashwell enclosure, maybe Dicey saw opportunities elsewhere. Denton was compensated to the tune of £50, the equivalent of two agricultural labourers' annual wages at the time, as well as being given the value of the farm crops. Dicey kept the coprolite plant and insisted,

"That in respect of a certain contract for the right to dig and search for coprolites on the land of Edward King Fordham at Ashwell entered into by the said Edward Dicey but not yet brought into active operation by him the said John Bailey Denton should release all his interests therein..."

(Ibid.)

Edward King Fordham was a man *of "remarkable ability, judgement and energy, and he steadily accumulated enormous power."* As the local magistrate, vice-chairman of the Board of Guardians and active member of the Vestry group and School Board he was well known. He owned the brewery on Mill Street in Ashwell which became the largest such concern in the neighbourhood. He had tied houses and customers in many local parishes and the diggers undoubtedly contributed to his wealth. (Davey, B.J. (1980), 'The Decline of a Village Economy', L.U.P. pp.38-39)

According to Clutterbuck, Dicey's agreement to work Fordham's land was on 30th April 1857. His labourers would have been keen to extract the shallower deposits on or just below the surface. They were then worked systematically across the fields until the increased depth made them uneconomic. Prices must have improved by 1859 as Kelly's Post Office Directory included a sentence for Ashwell which revealed the industry had really "taken off."

"On both sides of the river large beds of coprolites have been discovered; they are extensively worked, and after undergoing some chemical change form the basis of a manure now largely used in agriculture."

(HCRO. 28252)

This addition to Ashwell's account was repeated in every edition of Kelly's Directory until 1895 by which time it stated that the beds were worked out. During the Ashwell Enclosure of 1857 - 64 several of the local gentry must have discussed how the agricultural potential of the local-area could be improved. Denton provided advice about drainage and coprolites. He had experience with Clutterbuck, the Fordhams as well as St. John's College, Cambridge, who also owned land in the parish.

One local figure, David Simons, (variously written as Symonds or Simmonds in the documents) had started raising them. Whether it was from his own fields or he had a contract to work someone else's land is not known. In March 1857 he was able to supply the Cambridge Manure Company with £20 worth of coprolites at thirty-three shillings (£1.65) a ton. This rate was twelve shillings (£0.60) a ton less than those being sold in Cambridge at the time. Whilst it could have been to win business it was acknowledged that Ashwell coprolites realised less than the Cambridge variety as they had a lower phosphate content. Truckloads laden with coprolites left Ashwell station on their way to the company's new works in Duxford. He supplied them until July 1860, by which time he had received £238.76, enough to purchase a small estate. (HCRO. 28250-1)

As shall be seen, Simons and Dicey were not the only contractors involved in the area. Evidence shows that John Bennet Lawes made a number of agreements with landowners in Ashwell and surrounding parishes and then arranged their transport to his chemical manure works on the Thames at Deptford. In time he expanded with a second works at Barking . Further evidence shows that in September 1860 Abraham Hart, the tenant of St. John's College's Kirby Manor Farm in Northfield, wrote to the Master.

"The parties have been done digging coprolites some few weeks but have not got all the land levelled for cultivation, and I cannot say when they will as no one is at work on it."

(St. John's Coll. Cambridge (SJC) Muniments Box 162 Ashwell)

When St John's College first got involved in the industry is uncertain. Their first documented agreement was in 1866. It seems that Hart had assistance with the above letter as in October, still expressing concern about getting his land prepared, he wrote again adding that *"thay have not got the crop of the copperlite land... neither have thay levled it hall at pressent."* (SJC. Mun. Box 162 Ashwell)

Although it was not revealed who the "parties" were, subsequent evidence shows that a number of local farmers, contractors and labourers were involved. Robert Ground, one of the earliest coprolite contractors in the county, who had been involved with the diggings on Coldham's Common in Cambridge since 1857, must have heard on the grapevine about the discovery in Ashwell. He wrote to St. John's College in November 1860, offering £40 to dig each acre or to give a royalty, if they preferred, of four shillings (£0.20) a ton. This was considerably less than the rates he was paying the City Corporation and, unaware of the going price, Mr Reyner, the college bursar, asked the advice of John Denton. Denton pointed out that the depth varied considerably but that, *"...many things concur to prevent the Ashwell coprolites being as valuable (to the landowner) as those of Cambridge."* (SJC. 423.2.27)

Prices for Cambridgeshire coprolites fluctuated. In 1858 average rates peaked at forty-eight shillings (£2.40) a ton. In 1859 they dropped 30% but in 1860 rose again forty-three shillings (£2.15). Denton acknowledged that their chemical composition was inferior, in that the content of phosphate of lime was lower than the coprolite being worked in the Cambridge area. This would reduce the amount manure manufacturers- were prepared to pay. They were also found at quite a distance from good transport which led to higher costs for the contractor and, therefore, less profitable. The railway had actually reached Ashwell by 1850, so for many cart and tumbril owners there was extra money to be made taking the fossils to Odsey mill or Ashwell station.

According to Clutterbuck's account of the drainage of his estate, Denton paid him the equivalent of £60 - £70 per acre in royalties. Denton told Mr Reyner of St. John's College that it was slightly less.

> "...the sum obtained ranges from £55 - £60. The number of tons per acre reaches 200. These data will help you to make your bargain. In the College land the seam lies at a depth gradually but greatly increasing arising from the sharpness of the angle of dip and you should therefore secure as wide an extent as you can with one provision for restoration."

(SJC. 423.2.28)

Many agreements included specific clauses on restoring the land to cultivation. When the work was completed the contractor had to replace drains, restore and level the topsoil. This was not always done according to the stipulations however as Mr Sale, a Hinxworth farmer, reported that once the digging had been finished,

> "The abundance of coltsfoot or cow parsley along hedges and in previously dug fields attests to the bad management of this part of the early workings."

(Kiln, A. (1979) 'The Coprolite Industry', Putteridge Bury College, p.48)

Robert Ground made the College an offer of only £40. It was duly refused and David Simons made them an offer. Perhaps Simons heard that Ground's offer had been refused as, two days later, he wrote again with a slightly improved offer. It reflected his urgency of winning the digging rights.

> "We have been trying Mr Hart's ground but we do not find them lay so well as we expected Thay seem to lay in pockets We have been told that thar is some very good ones aboute 5 acres in Mr Chapman Field be longs to your

Collage we should like a peace as we have a great call for Coperlites now we are not getting know higher price yet only we have good call we are giveing £45 - £50 per acre."

(SJC. 432.2.28)

The College bursar was slow in making a decision. Perhaps he hoped to get an even higher rate. In July 1861 his attention was probably drawn to the sale of land adjoining college property belonging to Samuel Blott. 10a.1r.24p. was auctioned, part freehold and the other copyhold land belonging to the Manor of Westbury Nernewts on their Northfield estate. Under Blott's instructions two lots, *"believed to contain a large quantity of COPROLITES-,"* were offered for sale at the Three Tuns on 11th July. (SJC. D423.2.35; Royston Crow (RC), 1st August, 1861) Who made the highest bid is unknown. Maybe it was Ground, Simons, or another contractor? Manure manufacturers-' demand increased and so did their prices. Over the 1860s the average price for Cambridgeshire coprolites increased nearly 50%. This resulted in better offers to landowners and it seems likely that the college would have let Mr Chapman's Field be dug.

Throughout the late-1850s the residents of the Mordens would have become accustomed to this open cast agricultural mining and, given the profits being made, farmers, landowners, labourers and anyone with an eye for investment would have taken a keen interest. As knowledge of the seam spread, it expanded field by field, towards Guilden Morden. When the census was taken in 1861 it revealed that Guilden Morden's population had actually fell by twenty-three to 903 but there were two local men involved. 21-year old Eli Pettengal, *"the foreman of Coprolites"*, lived on the High Street and 40-year old Henry Theobalds, a *"fossil labourer,"* lived on Church Street. Maybe they were working in the parish at the time or were involved in the nearby workings in Ashwell or Hinxworth. There was no indication of large numbers of men descending into this parish. Maybe some had moved to Steeple Morden as over the same period its population increased twenty-five to 913. Litlington's population fell 12% over the decade to 693 but, as in Steeple Morden, no one was described as involved. In Hinxworth the only person mentioned was 18-year old James

Bonus *"At the Coprolite Works"*. He came from Sutton in Beds and lodged on the High Street. There was no mention of anyone in Ashwell. (CCRO. 1861 census; HCRO. 1861 census) Could it have been that many of those described as agricultural or general labourers could have been working in the pits?

Local gossip in many parishes has it that gangs of itinerant labourers were involved, moving from parish to parish as the diggings progressed. Maybe they were railway navvies or gangs of Irish labour. If such a gang was at work here it may not have wanted to be included in the census. Also, as the diggings were often done over winter, they had moved onto agricultural work when it was taken in April. Rumour has it that there was animosity between the railway navvies and the coprolite diggers in the pubs, and that the fire in Ashwell was the result of a fight that went too far. As items of village gossip there must have been some incidents that stuck in peoples' memories but the fire predated the diggings and the railway was completed before the diggings started. (Author's conversation with Mrs Sclater, Abington Pigotts)

By early spring 1862 workings had started in the area north of Guilden Morden. Here, the junction of the gault clay with the chalk marl ran in a somewhat undulating line round the northeast of the parish and into Abington Pigotts. The coprolite seam must have been found close to the surface and their profitability led to land speculation. Land agents acting for local landowners advertising property in the local press hoping to get an increased price with its coprolite potential.

"15a. 0r.36p of Orchard Pasture and Arable Land with a Dwelling House, Barn, Stabling and Outbuildings situated at Little Green in Guilden Morden in the occupation of William Street at £36 per annum. The property is contiguous to land from which a large quantity of coprolites have been dug, and will be sold in one or two lots."

(RC, 1st February, 1862, p.369)

There was no indication who bought it but a number of coprolite contractors were working in the area and competition between them could have led to sums of about £100 per acre being paid. £1,500 was a veritable fortune compared to £36 per annum. Maybe Lawes, Colchester or Packard purchased it? All had agreements in the area at this time. By 1862 Colchester had opened workings in Abington Pigotts under the superintendence of Charles Cooper.

In the March of 1863 a gang of local coprolite labourers joined in the celebrations in honour of the marriage of the Prince of Wales to Princess Alexandra of Denmark. Many local landowners and farmers gave feasts and entertainments to their labourers but this year there was a great celebration held at Royston. After the day's festivities, the largest celebration took place in the Bull Hotel. Amongst the local gentry was Mr F.N. Fordham, one of the entrepreneurial Fordham family which had interests in banking, farming, brewing and also the coprolite digging. Late in the proceedings, he

"...proposed the health of their visitors, coupled with the name of Mr Cooper, the superintendent of the great coprolite works at Abington. (cheers) Mr Cooper hoped his presence was not an intrusion. When he knew his coprolite men were coming up to the Festival on Tuesday last, he begged of them to behave well, and he did his best from morning till night towards keeping the peace. He thanked them for drinking his health. (cheers) The Chairman remarked that, when he heard that the coprolite men were coming, he said he did not wish for their presence without Mr Cooper, but if he came, he cared not how many he brought with him. (cheers)"

(CUL. RC, 10th March 1863)

This confirms the poor reputation of some of the diggers! Evidence from later that year shows how at least one local landowner tried to deter diggers from following the path to the beer house. In an agreement dated 30th December, 1863 between Sir Charles Bedlam and the Fordham brothers of Ashwell it mentioned *"Charles Cooper and the other persons employing a large number of men and boys in raising and crushing coprolites in the parishes of Abington Pigotts and Bassingbourn."* Cooper wanted to erect a small building at the cost of £65 on Bedlam's land so that the coprolite diggers, *"may have access for the purpose of reading and receiving mental, moral and religious instructions and being supplied with tea, coffee and other unintoxicating refreshments."* Bedlam agreed but stipulated that, *"no drunken workers should be allowed on the premises or those possessing intoxicating liquor on their persons."* (CCRO. 56/20/54/6; Grove, R. op.cit.p.44; See O'Connor, B. (1999), 'The Dinosaurs on Bassingbourn Fen', Bernard O'Connor, Gamlingay)

Finishing work earlier than agricultural labourers and having Saturday afternoon off encouraged regular attendance at the public houses. Maybe some joined the local football and cricket times but others got up to no good. Their social life led one of Bassingbourn's residents to object. Samuel Hopkins, the village grocer and postmaster, as well as being deacon to Bassingbourn Congregational Church, reported how

> *...the discovery of coprolites... brought together a large influx of persons from all parts who were employed in digging them out of the earth. These persons were the refuse of society, and with few exceptions, were extravagant, intemperate, licentious, depraved and atheistical in their conduct. One of the principal employers was an avowed Infidel. By his example, by his distribution of pernicious writings and tracts, the minds of many became infected.*
>
> *The employment of these men (who are called Diggers) was lucrative. They earned much money, they required lodgings. Consequently they were spread all over the village and neighbourhood. Whenever they lodged, with a few exceptions, they caused a spiritual blight, the people became indifferent, careless in their attendances*

and unconcerned about their state; many who were hopeful characters fell away and gave evidence that an increase in riches is destructive of spiritual life.

To meet this gigantic evil, fresh evangelistic efforts were put forth, with the aid of surrounding friends, a large room was built for the use of these people for reading and instruction on week days and for divine service on the Sunday evenings, an evangelist was also employed to converse with them, or preach, distribute tracts and endeavour to restrain them, but drunkenness and immorality so awfully and universally prevailed that these efforts for their salvation were fruitless. Some of these characters would occasionally attend our services, one or two were brought under the power of the word and were added to the church.

To prevent the spread of infidelity Mr Harrison gave lecture series with the assistance of other visiting ministers. The increase of population by the opening of the coprolite pits and the widespread wickedness caused thereby made his position more trying than any of his predecessors experienced yet he ceased not to warn the wicked."

(MS of Samuel Hopkins, p.210ff, Deacon of Bassingbourn Congregational Church. Original in possession of the church, Xerox copies in Cambridge Collection and CUL.)

This concern resulted in a variety of responses by the more religious members of the community. Over in the Eversdens a young lady, Annie Macpherson, attempted some evangelical work amongst them.

"It was not easy for a timid woman to approach these rough characters... at first her efforts were received- with sneers and scoffing. Often she would spend hours in prayer before she could get enough courage to approach a gang of men or even say a word apart... Gradually she won a hearing and a quiet influence- among them...

(Birt, L. (1931), 'The Children's Home Finder,' p.14)

During her time in Cambridgeshire she paid visits to London where she attended a Church mission. This provided her with new resources for

> *...a new power was soon evidenced in Annie Macpherson's work among the coprolite diggers. Clubs, coffee rooms, evening classes, prayer meetings and mission services were carried on, not only in the evenings but at the dinner times in barns if no other place was available, or in the open fields. Many Cambridge- undergraduates took part. At first the speakers were always men; it was unthought of that a woman should speak publicly... Miss Ellice Hopkins, whose father was a distinguished mathematical tutor at Cambridge, came over to address the gatherings of coprolite diggers and villagers. Ere Annie Macpherson left Cambridgeshire the fossil strata had been almost worked out in that immediate neighbourhood so that only the labour of the regular population was required but the result of her efforts were far reaching. A temperate -, united band of pious young men had been gathered out, full of simple earnestness each seeking to work for God according to his measure of light time and talents."*

(Ibld.)

The Cambridge University Coprolite Visiting societies were set up to raise funds to print and distribute religious tracts among the diggers, hold prayer meetings, set up Temperance Societies, open coffee houses, reading rooms and "schools" where moral and religious instruction was given. In Steeple Morden the brewer's influence was counteracted by a determined evangelical effort of the Methodists. They had great revival campaigns in 1859 and 1870 and were active among the coprolite diggers. By the mid-1870s they had enlarged the chapel to provide a school, a library, and a vestry and were said to have 400 adherents, almost half the population in 1873 and 500 by 1885. (CIP, 2nd September 1960 p.9; CCRO. R60/7/1, pp.12-13)

Mr Cooper made a request to the Fordham's to erect a *"coffee house and reading room"* on their land in Bassingbourn. In a memorandum dated 16th January 1864, he was given permission to erect a building thirty feet long by eighteen feet wide (11.1m. by 6.3m.), and provide it with a stove, tables, forms and a closet or shelves for books. This was for the

> *"large number of Men and boys who were engaged in raising and washing coprolites in the parishes of Abington Pigotts and Bassingbourn."*
>
> (CCRO. R56/20/54/6)

Given that Mr Cooper was also a beershop keeper it must have been hard for him to comply with certain sections of his agreement. These stipulated that he had

> [2]*...to undertake to keep out anyone who was intoxicated, to see that no improper language, betting or gambling took place within the walls and to promise there was to be no sale of intoxicating liquors or beers.*
> *...to use his best endeavours to promote order and decorum during the continuance of any religious service or public reading or lecture that may from time to time take place within the building."*
>
> (Ibid.)

The costs of the room were met by some of the more philanthropic local landowners and contractors. William Colchester paid £20, John Edward Fordham £22, Charles Bedlam £10, H. Butlers £5, Packard & Co. £5 and James Lilley £3. (Ibid.) Evidence shows that most of these contributors had diggings on their land and would have wanted to be seen as showing concern for their labourers. The formal opening was reported in the Royston Crow.

> *"**BASSINGBOURN**. On Good Friday at 4pm. a Coffee and Reading Room which has been erected for the use of the men employed in the Coprolite Works in the neighbourhood was opened. Some gentlemen who had promoted the*

object attended as well as several of the men who are employed at the works. Mr J.E.G. Fordham (at whose suggestion the building was proposed to be raised) being requested to preside, said that the many sad cases of assault, drunkenness, and theft had come before the magistrates from some of the men who had been employed in the coprolite works, had led him and others to feel much for them, and this resulted in an endeavour to improve their condition. He (Mr Fordham) knew that those of them who wished to be quiet and orderly had no place of refuge to flee from the resort of the drunkard and the profane. Their friends therefore at no little trouble and expense, had arranged this room for them, and they trusted it would be a blessing to many who might use it. Books had been provided for their instruction and amusement. The Rev. J. Harrison then read part of the 15th chapter of St. Luke, a hymn by Newton was sung, "In evil long I took delight," and prayers were offered for the divine blessing of the undertaking. Afterwards Mr Thurnall and the other friends of the object briefly addressed the meeting."

(RC. 1st April,1864, p.483)

However, although it was designed to entice coprolite diggers from the ten or more beerhouses that had sprung up in Bassingbourn, the room subsequently declined into selling beer itself as the "Tally Ho." It was hardly surprising given the occupations of the Fordhams and Mr Cooper. It can still be recognised as the long bay projecting from a grey-brick house, next to the house that used to be the V.G store on the corner of South Road. Several other beerhouses were opened for the diggers. These included "The John O' Gaunt" and "The Fountain." A barn on the Eyeworth road at Mobb's Hole Farm acted as a dormitory and kitchen for some of the diggers. The farmhouse also acted as a beerhouse, known as the "Labour in Vain." The farmer and Ernest Fordham as brewery owner, capitalised on the thirst of the diggers after a hard day's work at the pits. This was opened especially for the diggers, and, as expected, closed when the diggings ceased. Where Flecks Lane meets North Brook End a public house called "The Diggings" was erected for the coprolite diggers. It too may have been built by the Fordhams. (CCRO. R60/7/1 p.33; 296/SP 1163; RC 10th July 1885.) Members of the Congregational church erected a tin chapel near Wendy where services were held and attempts were made to evangelise amongst the men. Non-attenders called it "The Tin Tabernacle" and the barn used at Boy Bridge was called "Bible Grove". (CC 12th January 1877; Agricultural History Review, vol. xxiv, p.42; Pelling, E.J. Bassingbourn School Centenary 1877-1977, (pamphlet 1977) p.1)

Following the 1863 enclosure of the land north of Ashwell in which Edward Fordham got the best land he arranged the construction of "Elbrook House". It was built in forty acres of parkland just north of the village and paid for in part from his coprolite and brewing revenues. (Davey, B.J. op.cit. p.39)

In the Cambridgeshire fens where gang labour was common there were many reports of child abuse. A ganger would take a large number of children out into the fields to work for the day. It was the accepted practice for parents to take their children to work with them. So, when father got a job at the diggings, sons went along too. Many children were employed in the coprolite works to help with the washing and sorting but girls only tended to be engaged on piecework where there were large quantities of gravel and unwanted larger stones found in the bed. The census shows no evidence of female employment in this area but as that particular job tended to be done over winter it could have been that they had other work to do at the time the enumerator came round.

Employing children was accepted. It increased profits for the contractors as it reduced labour costs by up to 50%. Concern about the situation spread. With no compulsory schooling huge numbers of children in the urban areas were being employed in factories, mines and mills or as domestics above and below stairs. Fred Watts, of Cheyney Street, left school at nine unable to write and by eleven earned eighteen shillings (£0.90) a week sorting flints from the coprolites. (Mary Murfitt, CCRO. R60/7/1)

In 1866 the government set up a commission to investigate the employment of children, young persons and others in agriculture. Rev. J. B. James, the rector of Gamlingay, provided fascinating details of conditions in the local coprolite workings. He wrote to Hon. E. Portman, the commissioner in charge of the government's investigations.

"The coprolite diggings in our neighbourhood have occupied very many of our boys, many of whom earn at them 8s. and 9s. a week, which is more than the farmers can give them."

SANDY.

50. Mr Coulson. - "Girls of 7 years up to 18 years are employed in the coprolite works. The work is taken by the piece; they get a sum per ton for picking over the fossils. A girl of ten years would earn 7s. a week by day work, but much more by piece work. The state of education among them is very low; some can read, hardly any can write. The parents also are very uneducated. This and the adjoining district of Polton [sic] is a gardening tract; children are much employed in large numbers in peeling onions and such like work. I have seen gross cases of immorality and indecency, even among the smaller children, at leisure moments at the coprolite mills when waiting for the carts, and have heard much bad language, which is readily learnt by the young from constantly hearing it round them. The foremen do not check them. The sexes should be separated at the mills, by means of different sheds, or even by separate mills for boys and girls. In one instance the foreman keeps a public house, where the wages are paid, and the men and children are allowed to have as much drink as they like during the week on credit, and the money is deducted on pay night. These children have no time for learning, except in the evening."

ARLESEY

46a. "There are three sets of coprolite works, three brickyards and a cement works, which have caused a great increase in population, especially in summer, when

Lower Cretaceous Terrestrial Communities

a *Iguanadon* (Vertebrata: Reptilia: Archosaur – dinosaur)
b *Megalosaurus* (Vertebrata: Reptilia: Archosaur – dinosaur)
c *Hypsilophodon* (Vertebrata: Reptilia: Archosaur – dinosaur)
d *Acanthopholis* (Vertebrata: Reptilia: Archosaur – dinosaur)
e *Equisetites* (Pteridophyta: Calamites – horsetails)

(McKerrow, W.S.. (1978), *The Ecology of Fossils: An Illustrated Guide*,
Duckworth, p.297)

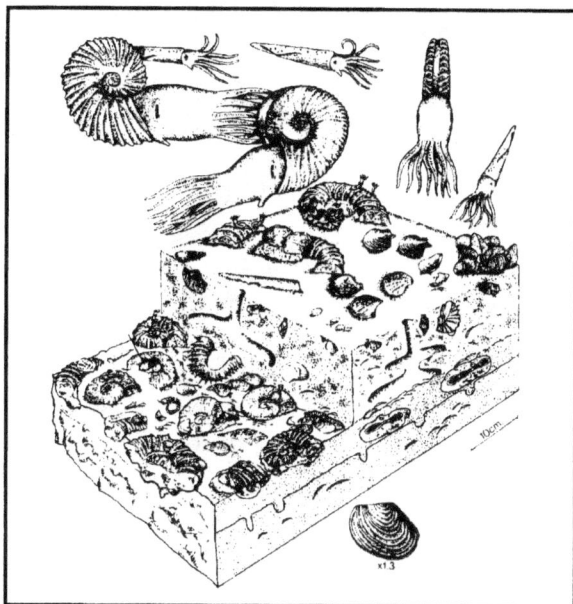

The Phosphate bed Community
(McKerrow, W.S.. (1978), *The Ecology of Fossils: An Illustrated Guide,*
Duckworth, p.286)

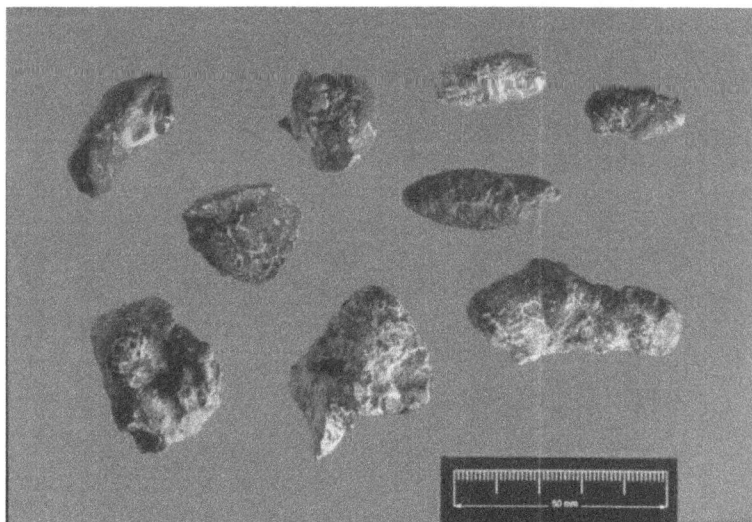

Cambridgeshire coprolites. (Photograph courtesy of Earth
Sciences Museum, Cambridge)

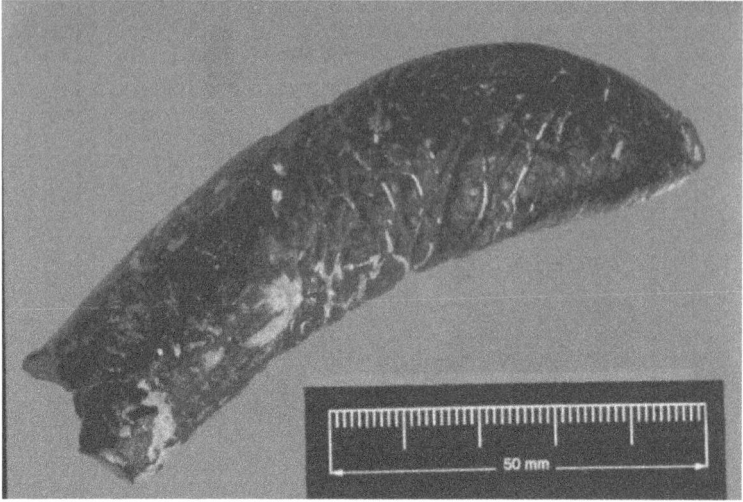

The Barrington coprolite
(Photograph courtesy of Earth Sciences Museum, Cambridge)

Lawes' Chemical Manure Company, Deptford Creek (Spring Circular for Lawes' Manures 1864, Rural History Centre, Reading University)

North

- Coprolite workings
o Location of Coprolite labourers
■ Manure Works

Stretham
Soham
Wicken
Upware
Reach
BURWELL
Swaffham Prior
Swaffham Bulbeck
Bottisham
Cottenham
Waterbeach
Horningsea
Lode
Stow-cum-Quy
Milton
Fen Ditton
Westwick
Chesterton
CAMBRIDGE
Cherry Hinton
Coton
Grantchester
Fulbourn
Madingley
Trumpington
Barton
O'Teversham
Comberton
Haslingfield
Hauxton
Great Shefford
Harlton
Harston
Little Shefford
Kingston
Newton
Great Eversden
Orwell
Barrington
DUXFORD
Little Eversden
Foxton
Wimpole
Shepreth
Thriplow
Croydon
Meldreth
Fowlmere
Wendy
Knapwell
Wrestlingworth
Whaddon
Bassingbourn
Gamlingay
Abington Pigotts
Melbourn
ROYSTON
Litlington
Everton
Steeple Morden
Himxworth
Sutton
Guilden Morden
Ashwell
Potton
Edworth
Ashwell Station
Astwick
Henlow
Stotfold
Shefford
Arlesey
Campton
Meppershall
Upper Stondon
Clophill
Gravenhurst
Lower Stondon
Upper
Shillington
Pirton
Highant Gobion
Barton-Le-Clay
Ampthill
Millbrook
Ridgmont
Eggington
Stanbridge
Billington
Edlesborough
Slapton
Leighton Buzzard
Brickhill
Ditton
Bishopstone

49

Coprolite Diggings at Orwell, Cambridgeshire. 1860s – 1870s
(Courtesy of Cambridgeshire Collection W27.1J80 25358)

Coprolite Diggings in Cow Pasture, Abington Pigotts, Cambridgeshire, 1883
(Courtesy of Mr and Mrs Sclater, Abington Pigotts)

HORSE-POWERED COPROLITE WASHMILL

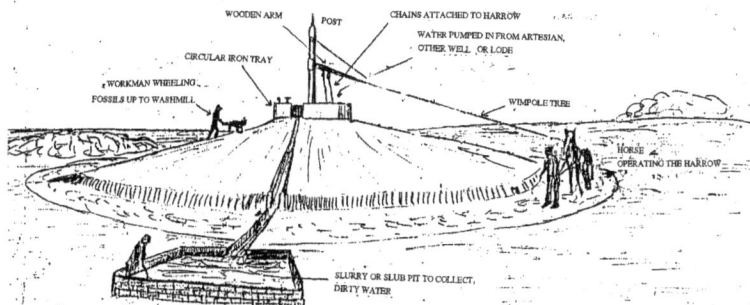

(Based on sketch in Richard Grove's Cambridgeshire Coprolite Mining Rush)

Undated photograph of a circular coprolite harrow
Cambridgeshire Collection: W27.1. KO. 19554).

Steam engine hauling coprolites from Whaddon to Shepreth Station c.1880
(Cambridge Collection Q AR J8 11029 Courtesy of Mrs Coningsby, Whaddon

Undated postcard of horse-drawn tumbrils carrying coprolites to the railway station at Millbrook, Bedfordshire.

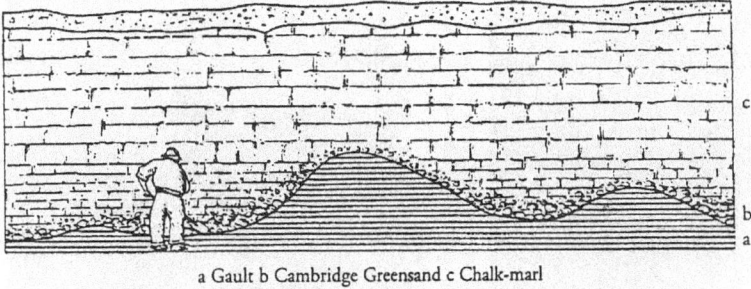

a Gault b Cambridge Greensand c Chalk-marl

View of a coprolite pit in Horningsea, Cambs.
(Jukes-Browne, A.J. & Hill, W. *Cretaceous Rocks of Britain,* Mem. Geol. Surv. 1903, p.194)

Undated photograph of coprolite diggers in Orwell, Cambridgeshire
(Courtesy of Sue Miller, Orwell History Society)

Photographs of the coprolite works on Sandy Heath, Bedfordshire, c.1882) The top photo shows women outside the sorting shed. The lower photographs shows a horse-powered cylindrical washmill. (Courtesy of Potton History Society)

Caricature of J.B. Lawes who patented the technique of dissolving coprolite and other phosphatic materials in sulphuric acid to produce superphosphate. He set up his own manure company, won contracts to raise coprolites and purchased others from diggings across south-east England (*Vanity Fair* 8th July 1882)

Undated photograph of Edward Packard (1819 – 1899) who
founded Edward Packard and Company. In 1843 he began making superphosphate by dissolving old bones in sulphuric acid at Snape Mill. In
1851 he built Britain's first complete sulphuric acid and superphosphate
works at Bramford and went on to win coprolite agreements and purchase coprolites from across southeast England.
(http://www.yara.com/en/about/yara_centennial/heritage/
fisons_inter.html)

1861 photograph of William Colchester (1813–1898), one
of the first manure manufacturers to use Suffolk coprolites.
Had manure works in Ipswich, moved into Cambridgeshire
fens in 1846, won coprolite contracts and purchased others
from diggings across southeast England.
(Courtesy of Giles Colchester)

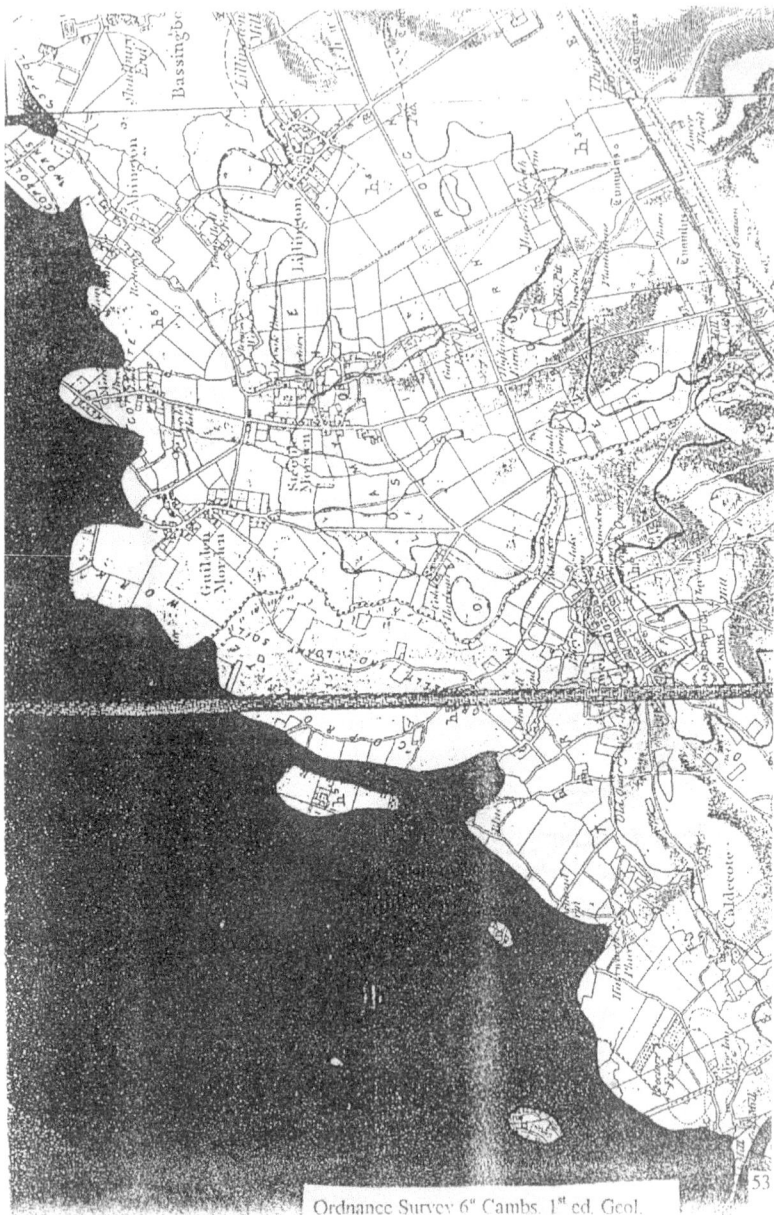

Ordnance Survey 6" Cambs. 1st ed. Geol.

Plan of coprolite field at Little End

(St John's College, Muniments Box 162 Ashwell)

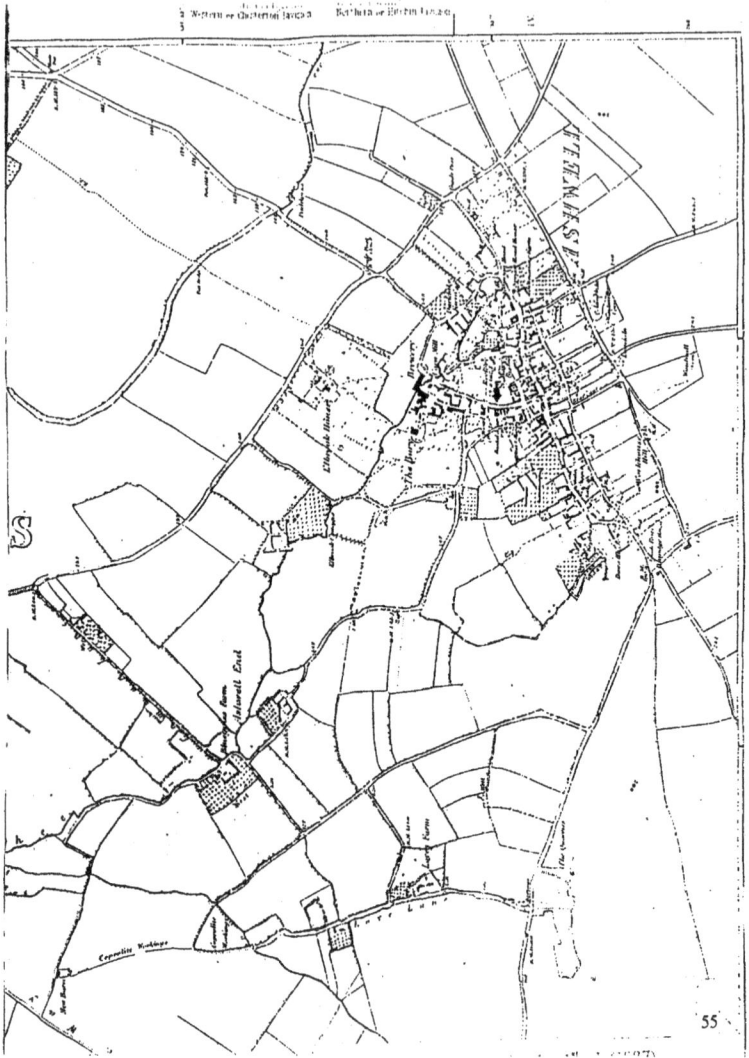

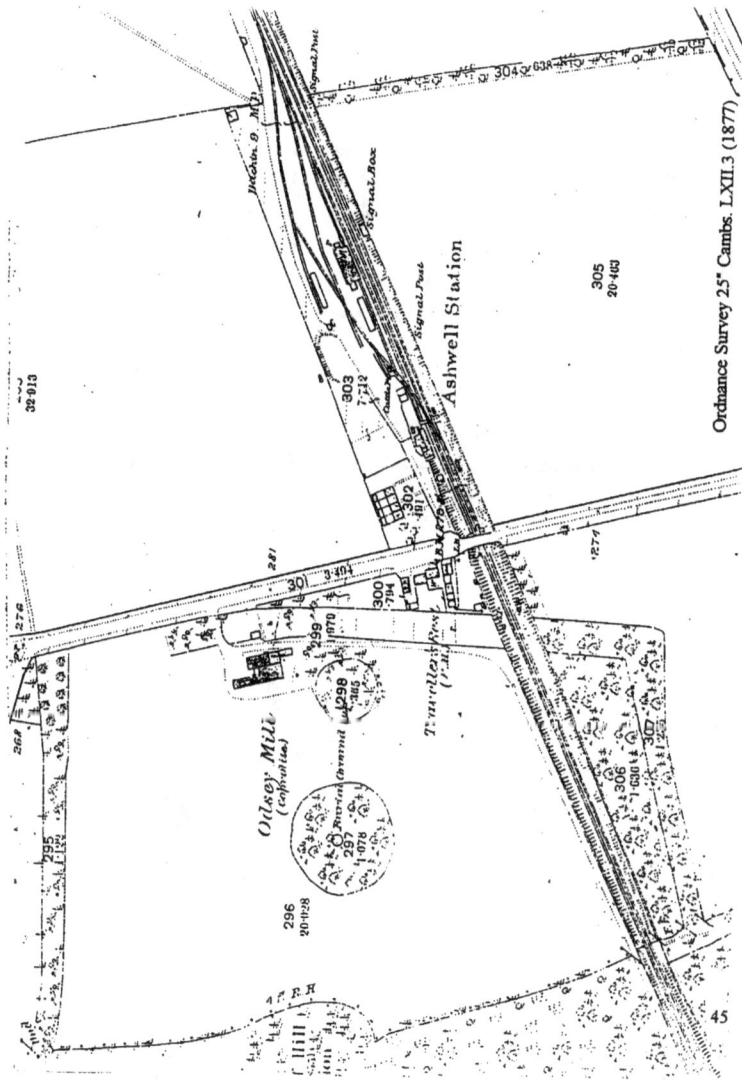

Ordnance Survey 25" Cambs. LXII.3 (1877)

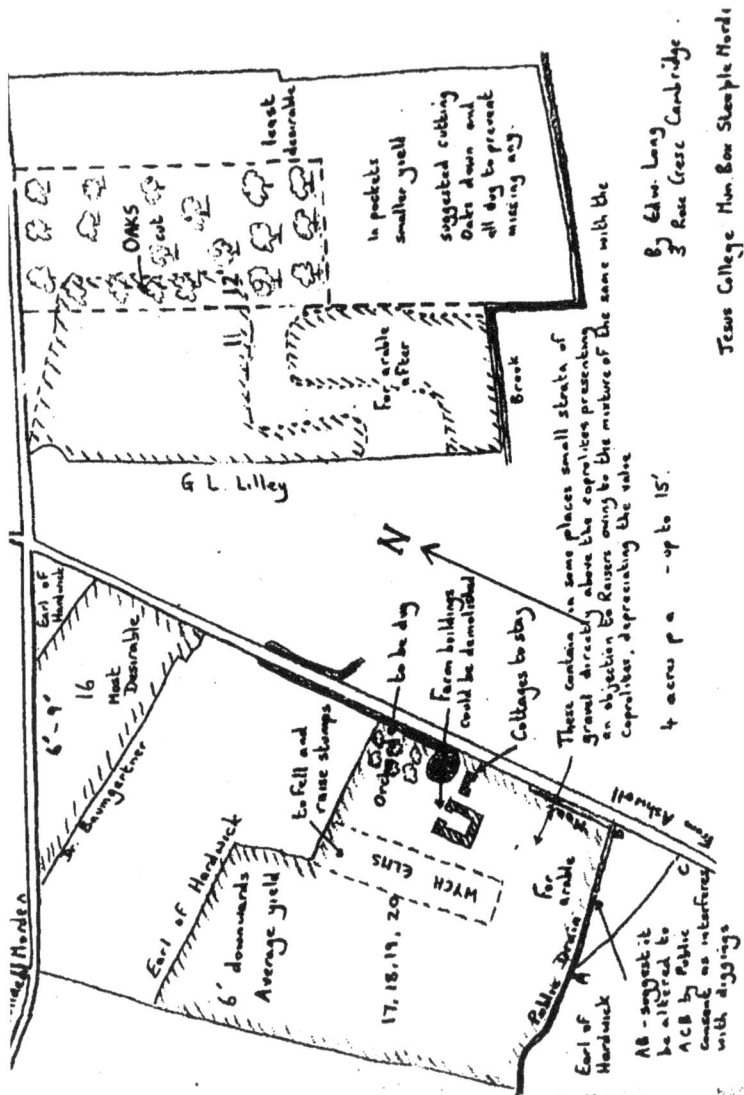

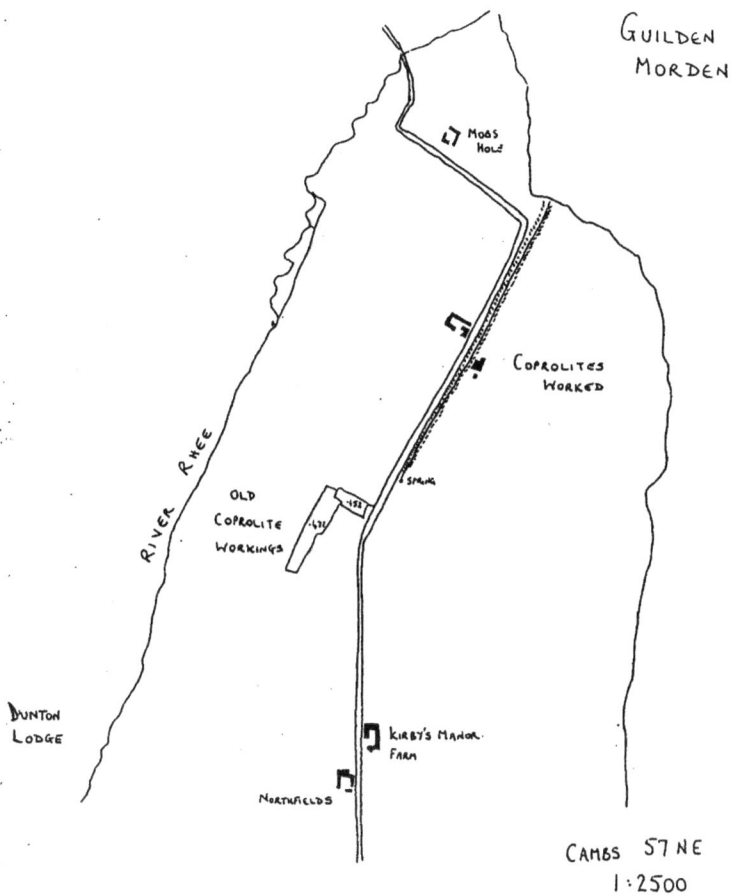

GUILDEN
MORDEN

MOAS
HOLE

COPROLITES
WORKED

RIVER RHEE

SPRING

OLD
COPROLITE
WORKINGS

DUNTON
LODGE

KIRBY'S MANOR
FARM

NORTHFIELDS

CAMBS 57 NE
1:2500

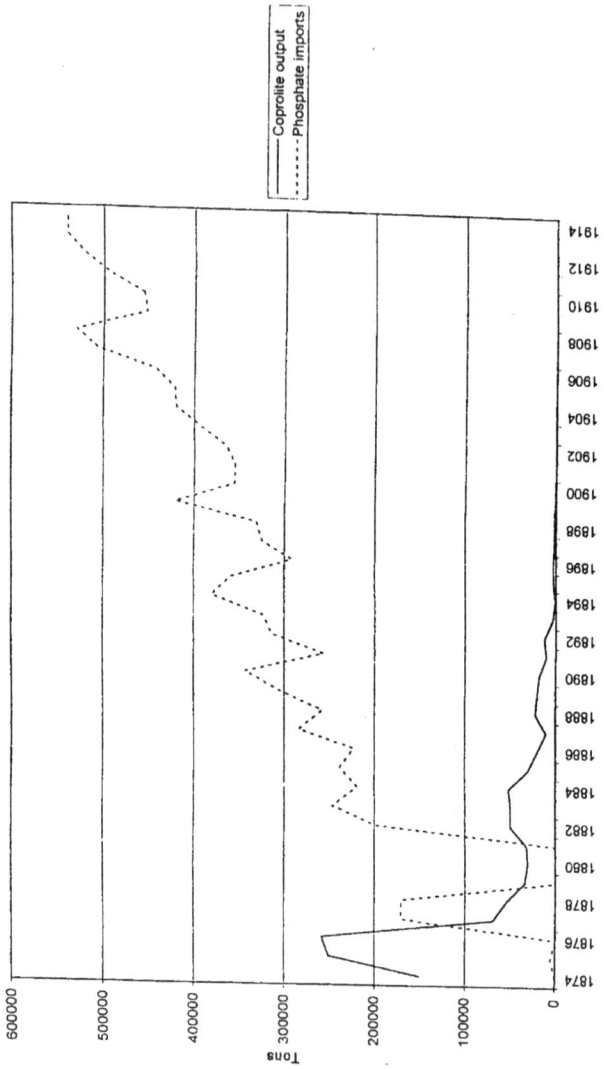

Coprolite Production and Phosphate Imports 1874-1914

many houses are crowded. Coprolite employs a good many men, many of whom are strangers. Coprolite works employ some boys, leading horses.
BIGGLESWADE UNION.
"Coprolite works and brick fields may be added to the causes given by Mr Weale for the overcrowding and use of bad cottages in the neighbourhood of Biggleswade."

(BCRO. CRT 160/140 Parliamentary Papers 1867-8 XVII '1st Report of the Commissioners on the Employment of Children, Young Persons and others in Agriculture', pp. 343, 506, 518)

Mr Postman's summary added further details about the work and showed that the local MP and landowner, Arthur Peel, of Sandy Lodge, had attempted to provide the youngsters with the rudiments of education.

COPROLITE DIGGINGS.
"131. There is in Cambridgeshire much employment for the young of both sexes of the agricultural labouring classes at the coprolite works. These works are increasing in number, the price paid for the right of digging is from £80. to £100. an acre, it being agreed that the land shall be restored to the owner levelled and in a state fit for cultivation. The digging work is done by men and grown lads; boys are employed in wheeling barrows, and children of both sexes in sorting the fossils in the mills. Wages are high, boys can earn 8s. and 9s. a week, and a girl of 10 years of age earns 7s.a week by day work, but more by the piece, the payment for picking over the fossils being usually so much per ton... The state of education among these children is very low, and testimony is given as to the existence of gross immorality and indecency, no care being taken to separate the sexes at the mills."

(Ibid. p.108)

As there was no provision for toilets some workers probably went behind the nearest hedge. The problem of young people was not completely solved until the introduction of the 1870 Education Act which made schooling compulsory. The money being realised by landowners and contractors was considerable and led some of the local gentry to attempt to rate the coprolite works. All local businesses had to contribute to the parish's Poor Relief. This was an early form of social security set up by Elizabeth I to ensure parishes provided for those parishioners in need.

"GUILDEN MORDEN. *Coprolite Works. - A correspondent from this village, who rejoices in the prejudices having been got over with respect to taking from the earth the great mineral deposits, says that, "no doubt in a short time the legislature will enable the inhabitants, when coprolite works are going on, to rate them, both to "the relief of the poor" and to the "surveyor's rate." We have reason to believe these are rateable at once without any interference of the legislature, and that a parish in the county has laid the matter before Mr Naylor, the barrister, in order to rate these works."*

(CC,17th October,1863,p.8)

No evidence has emerged that shows whether local parishes did succeed in rating them. Maybe investigation of church records will reveal it. Contractors expressed considerable opposition to being rated. They claimed that the "diggings" was only a temporary use of the land and that they should therefore be exempt. It was not until eight years later that Mr Naylor eventually found against them. (Leighton Buzzard Observer,17th January 1871) Horse-powered coprolite mills were rated at £50 and steam-driven ones at £100. When brickyards owners were only paying £5 per annum one can understand the contractors' concerns but also just how profitable they were compared to other extractive industries.

As the working of the nodule bed on Ashwell Northfield gradually progressed north and north-eastwards into Abington Pigotts, it became apparent to St. John's College's land agents that the deposit also ran under their estate in Steeple Morden. Suspecting that Rev. G. Pigotts of Abington Pigotts had sold coprolite land in North Brook End that adjoined college property Mr Reyner wrote to him on November 16th 1863.

> *"If I'm correctly informed you have sold some in an adjoining field. If so would you kindly inform me*
> *1. What royalty you receive per acre?*
> *2. Whether in addition the purchaser compensates your tenant and if so what amount per acre?. 3. At what time the agreement was made?"*
>
> (St. John's College Muniments Box. 162)

An afterthought led the bursar to add a second letter in that day's post asking Rev. Pigott how many tons per annum were obtained and what royalty was paid to the landowner. Perhaps the impersonal tone of the communication led to Rev. Pigotts replying the next day that he was unable to supply the information as "...*your informant is wrong in supposing I have sold any land in North Brook End.*" (St. John's Estate Box 162) News of the college's interest in having the coprolites raised came to the attention of Herbert Fordham. He was acquainted with the contractors of the Great Eastern Railway, which was extended to Cambridge during the early-1850s, a connection that allowed him to secure the coal trade between London and Peterborough. It was his obituary in the Royston Crow of 1891 that revealed his relationship with the 4th Earl of Hardwick, who was Lord-in-Waiting to Queen Victoria.

> *"Mr Fordham was one of the first to recognise the importance of the coprolite deposits in the Cam valley, and his engineering ability led him early into the work of raising the coprolites on a large scale. With wise foresight he arranged to purchase the sole right of digging over a large part of Lord Hardwicke's estate and succeeded beyond his expectations. Mr. Fordham followed up this step by converting his flour mill at Odsey into a coprolite grinding mill, shortly afterwards adding*

the manufacture of artificial manures. His practical experience as a large farmer aided him in the development of this business."

(Royston Crow, 1st May, 1891)

Writing from "Odsey Mills, Manure and Coprolite Works" he sent a letter to Reyner a week later.

"I understand your College has some coprolite ground for sale at Little Morden and as I have some large works adjoining I should be glad of the offer of it."

(St. John's Coll.Mun.Box.162)

This was declined as a few weeks later Reyner was approached by Swann Jepps Wallis, a Duxford coprolite merchant who had workings in many of the villages on the coprolite belt. He offered them £80 per acre and gave the bursar of King's College as a reference. This seemed to clinch the deal over Mr Fordham, who must have been raising them from the Earl of Hardwick's land in this area. Where his adjoining works were is uncertain as no further documentation of them has emerged. A formal agreement was written up and on 6th January 1864 Wallis was given permission to raise them from the 7a.3r.11p. field shown on the map in the illustrations. Wallis engaged Abraham Pearman as his foreman, who took on a gang of men and got started at Michaelmas. Maybe the seam ran too deep as college records show that his men had only worked 1a.2r.0p. by January 1869.

The increase in road traffic associated with the diggings brought complaints from some of the rate-paying gentry. They expressed concern about the poor state of the roads. The wheels of the heavily laden carts threw up mud leaving deep ruts after the wet weather. It was particularly bad near the new Railway Bridge on the Old North Road, which had only been completed in 1860. At their first meeting in 1863 the Kneesworth and Caxton Turnpike Committee

"Ordered that the surveyor do obtain 13 tons of granite for the repairs of the road near the Old North Road Railway Station and 50 yards of gravel for the south end of the road;

Ordered that the clerk write to the secretary of the Bedford and Cambridge Railway Company to complain of the unsatisfactory state of the railway bridge at the Old North Railway Station and the approaches thereto.

Ordered that in consequence of the increase in traffic occasioned by the opening of the Bedford and Cambridge Railway and the Coprolite works, notice be given in due course to the holder of the tolls of our intention to defer to the existing lease at the end of the present term.

The surveyor was ordered to employ a fit person to be stationed at or near the Old Road Railway Station for the purpose of ascertaining the amount of traffic as a guide for the erection of a new toll gate near that station."

(CCRO. 1863 T/k/AH3 Kneesworth and Caxton Turnpike)

The steam engines hauling truckloads of washed coprolites made such a noise that one frightened the horse of Charles Hales, the farmer mentioned earlier. He was thrown and the accident was reported in the Cambridge Chronicle as *"a fall which had nigh proved fatal."* (Cambridge Chronicle (CC), 18th July 1863) Two months later another accident on the road from Kneesworth to Royston was reported. George Smith was driving his wife and daughter in a gig when *"within a half a mile of the village the horse took fright at the engine which had been for some hours unable to proceed."* The noise and the clouds of steam as the fire was stoked up again made the horse bolt. The gig overturned and its occupants were thrown out. The daughter was bruised, Mrs Smith had three teeth broken and *"poor George"* readers were told, *"lay in a state of insensibility"* until Mr Pyne, the Royston surgeon, arrived. The editor commented *"Surely the government ought to do something to prevent these traction and other engines passing along our roads, not only to the annoyance but also the danger of the public."* (CC 17th October 1863)

The solution to the problem was for the trustees of the turnpikes, the body responsible for the maintenance of the public roads, to use the powers of the 1861 Locomotive Act to prohibit any steam-powered engines from the roads except between the hours of midnight and six in the morning. (CUL. Add.Ms.6017, Arrington Turnpike Trust; Trustees of Hauxton Roads, 2nd October 1863) This limited the steam engines to hauling trucks or "bogeys" along specially laid tramways to the roadside and provided a considerable boost to the local carting industry. Great piles of coprolites would have been seen by the roadside ready for the carters to load onto their tumbrils. As coprolite yields averaged 250 tons an acre tens of thousands of tons would have been carried to the railway station. (Kingston, A., (1889), 'Old and New Industries on the Cam.' Warren Press, Royston p.16) Observant Victorian train spotters would have noticed numerous drop-sided wooden railway trucks with COPROLITES painted on the side being pulled by steam train to manure factories in London or Ipswich.

Whilst horse and cart transport would have increased there were still accidents involving coprolite trucks. Fred Sillence, a local historian, recalled how an article in the Royston Crow reported how one coprolite contractor, rather than a use a horse or a more expensive steam engine, had cut costs by using men to haul the trucks.

> "...the rails for which ran behind two cottages at the end of Shedbury (sic) Lane. The trucks had ropes at each end, and would be pulled along by two men, with another man pushing. This and digging in the actual pits, which were some ten feet deep in unstable soil, could be dangerous to the workmen and tragedies were not unknown. My friend recalls one such instance: "My grandfather's brother was aged 26, and his friend was 22 when they were killed together - they were run over by one of the trucks while on coprolite work, on October 19th 1869. They were buried together in Bassingbourn churchyard."
>
> (RC, 26th April, 1991)

More details of the actual workings were revealed in Audrey

Kiln's interviews with some of the old diggers. Ashwell diggers were paid from three halfpennies to three pence (£0.006 - £0.027) for removing each cubic yard and a good digger could earn up to thirty and forty shillings (£1.50 - £2.00) a week, piece-rate. Mr Street of Hinxworth described the spades they used.

> "...the shaft was of metal, about two foot long and a wooden T-shaped handle, about 5 inches wide, was fixed into the top of this. The blade was narrow, the top being about four inches, narrowing to 2 inches, with an overall length of 6 inches."
>
> (Kiln. op.cit. pp.43-4)

Mr. Street started coprolite work with his father when he was only ten and his task was to sort out the washed stones and remove such items as stones or pebbles unacceptable by the manure manufacturers. He claimed that women and girls were also engaged to do this sorting for what was the comparatively low wages of only three shillings (£0.15) a week.

> "To avoid cutting their hands on the sharp-edged shells they used a wooden scraper to push the coprolites from side to side. Refuse was thrown over their shoulders and any items of interest, such as sharks' teeth, were collected and sold to supplement their earnings."
>
> (Ibid.p.38)

Another Hinxworth man, William Sale, remembered when he was

> "...transferred to the job of sifting and carrying away the earth removed by the diggers. It was customary to have young lads working at the bottom of the trenches in order to handle this work, part of which involved loading and carrying a three stone tin of fossils up the planks to the pit top for removal to the washing mill. He was twelve, and his wages had been increased to the munificent sum of 5/- per week...
> The boys worked in pairs, one pair to a digger and they

were kept very busy. Their day started at 8am. and they finished for the evening at 6pm. They were allowed half an hour for lunch and worked a six-day-week. Referring to those times as "the good old days", he said that had he been working on the land, his average wage would have been 2/- per day. When one realises that at that time the national average wage for adult men engaged in agriculture was 8/- to 10/- per week, it is little wonder that the local men preferred to work the pits than the land.

On wet days, the boys practised walking the planks, imitating the skilled barrow runners and preparing for the time when, as adults, they would take their place as runners. The less experienced men usually started working at the bottom 'kench', where there was little fear of falling from the planks when the soil was being shifted. As the men gained more experience they were promoted to higher 'kenches', where the work was obviously more risky. The layers of coprolite were dug out by shovel or crowbar and care had to be taken to watch the sides of the trenches for cracks. Mr. Street said that collapses were fairly frequent and sometimes men became trapped beneath fallen earth. It was customary to have a man standing on the top of the trench watching the sides, ready to shout a warning to those below at the first sign of trouble. The depth of the pits varied from as little as 12 feet, but 20 feet was considered about the normal depth both for the safety of the men and for the economics involved.

Mr. Sale told of the horse-play that used to go on among the more experienced diggers, much to the consternation of those below apparently. "I was told of men who actually stood on their heads on the uppermost planks and of one man who actually used to cartwheel along the length of the top plank. Mr. Street couldn't remember an incidence of a barrow falling off."

(Ibid. pp.40-41)

However, there were numerous accidents in the pits. On Henry George Fordham's visits to his family's workings he observed some dangerous working methods. He was concerned enough to write to the editor of the Cambridge Chronicle: -

ACCIDENTS AT THE COPROLITE DIGGINGS.

"Sir, - I write to call your attention to the frequency of accidents at the coprolite diggings. Within the last week three fatal cases have come to my notice, and besides these we hear daily of men and boys having their limbs broken and their backs strained, and thus being reduced to idleness and deprived of their wages for weeks and even months together. We used not to hear of these accidents when coprolite digging first became an institution in this county, because the operations were performed in the natural straightforward manner, but now, to save time and money, it has become the practise to dig a trench some 8 or 10 feet deep and then to undermine till the earth falls in and finally to shovel it into the barrow. Of course, unless timely warning is given of the approaching fall of earth, and unless the men immediately avail themselves of the warning, accidents cannot but occur. It was formerly universally the practice to have two men on watch in order to give warning, but now to save more time and more money, in many cases even this necessary precaution is abolished. Doubtless in many cases this is neglected simply through the carelessness of the workmen, but surely the foreman ought not only to say that the workmen may do it but to see that they do it. If the system of watching is not sufficient to prevent accidents, I should think it would be possible to have a simple system of props to prevent the fall of earth until they were removed, and if they were to prove insufficient or impractible, then I say we ought to give up the present method of digging, and revert to the old practice, for, as we all know how profitable the coprolite pits are, it would not be too much to expect that the proprietors would give up a small portion of their profits to save the lives of their workmen. I hope that the proprietors will consider if something may not be done, and that they will not continue, in order to save a few pounds, to sacrifice

the limbs and lives of their fellow creatures.
I am, Sir, Yours faithfully, H.G.F."

(CC, Nov.16th 1864)

In the August of 1863 William Elbourn, the landowner of land in the fen near the Abington Pigotts coprolite works hoped to increase its value by referring to the presence of the coprolites. He arranged the sale of

"9a.3r.12p. of Highly Productive ARABLE LAND situate in the Fen, abutting West (by means of a driftway forming part thereof) on to the Parish Road and known to contain a RICH BED of Coprolites."

(RC. 1st August, 1863)

Evidence shows that it was purchased by one of Mr Colchester's competitors, Edward Packard and Company, another Ipswich firm of manure manufacturers. Their agent in the Cambridge area was Nathaniel Johnson who must have felt it worthwhile that the company gained a foothold in this area of extensive and higher quality coprolites than those being raised in Suffolk and the fens. They also wanted to compete with Mr Colchester. In October Clement Francis, was engaged by Mr Elbourn to draw up terms. Packard was allowed to occupy the land for three years at a royalty of only £50 an acre - a very low rate. These might well have been the workings referred to in Mr Francis' notebook as being near Bleak Hall. (CCRO. Francis Bill Books A-N 1863 pp.347, 362; Whitaker, N. (1921), 'Water Supply of Cambs.' MGS, London, p.53)

On the 24th February 1864, this development prompted Mr J.H. Fordham, of Ashwell, who owned adjoining land being farmed by Mr Elbourn, to arrange the sale of twenty-one acres of *"Highly Productive Land lying in the Fen and believed to contain a valuable BED OF COPROLITES."* (RC. 1st December 1863, 1st February,1864) Faced with this competition Mr Colchester purchased the plot.

In autumn 1864, the vicar of Guilden Morden, shed light on their discovery. In his report to the bishop he indicated that the main centre of operations was still in Ashwell.

"Much of the land has been underdrained in the last four years, the tenants finding labour and the lessees pipes... The population is 906. Straw plaiting is carried on and at present many persons are employed in digging coprolites which are found in the Greensand formation in the south of the parish."

(CCRO. Church Comm. files, Guilden Morden,1984)

Henry George Fordham was a fellow of the Geological Society and built up a collection of fossils found in the local pits. How much he paid for the better specimens is not known but several shillings could buy a good piece on the stall on Cambridge market. He wrote a paper on his finds which was published in the 1866 Proceedings of the Geological Association.

"The position of the Greensand in the pits made to obtain the nodules, viz. at the bottom, makes it almost impossible to collect from the bed in situ, and, as the marl when thrown up is generally immediately removed to the washing mill, almost the only way to obtain fossils is to search the heaps of washed nodules; this mode of collecting is in many respects unsatisfactory, as the fragile shells are broken and destroyed in the washing mill, and all the specimens suffer attrition. It must also be born in mind that the proportionate quantity of fossils must be greater when compared with the heaps of nodules (which themselves form perhaps 1/20th or less of the whole deposit), when compared with the entire mass of the bed itself. I have had, however, on one occasion, when some of the marl was dug up and left for some months exposed to the atmosphere, an opportunity of obtaining some of the more fragile specimens, and of getting more accurate idea of the comparative rarity of different species.

LIST OF FOSSILS FROM THE UPPER GREENSAND, MORDEN AND ASHWELL.

LIST OF FOSSILS FROM THE UPPER GREENSAND, MORDEN AND ASHWELL.

REPTILIA-
Ichthyosaurus campylodon -
lanciformis-
Teeth, vertebrae, and fragments of
 other bones. Not very common.
  Polyptychodon-
        Teeth. Rare.
  Plesiosaurus-
        Vertebrae. Rare
        Otodus appendiculatus-
        Teeth. Common.
      MOLLUSCA-
  Cephalopoda-
  Ammonites rostratus. Rather common.
Very common.
  A. cratus. Rather Common
costatus. Very rare.
   A.caelonotus. Rather common.
   A. pachys. Rare.
   Hamites. Rare.

common.
   Baculites. Rare. T. obtusa. Rare.
   Belemnites minimus. Common.

rare.
   B. ultimus. Rather common.
   Gasteropoda-

   Pleurotomaria (?rodani, D'Orb.)

      Rather common

   P. Brongniartianum. Rare.

PISCES -
Saurocephalus

Teeth, Rare.
Edaphon-
Fragments. Rare
Gryodus-
Palatal teeth. Very rare.
Lamma- Teeth. Common

Vertebrae. Rather rare.
MOLLUSCA-
Lamellibranchiata-
 Avicula gryphaeoides.

  Pecten quinque-

MOLLUSCOIDA-
Brachiopoda-
Terebratula biplicata.
        Very

T. semiglobosa.(?)
        Rather

T. ovata. Rather rare.
Terebratulina gracilis.
        Common.
Terebratella. (kingena)
        lima. Rare.
Rhynchonella. sulcate.
        Rare.
R. lineolata var.
   Carteri. Very rare.

P. semiconcava. Very rare.

P. Gibbsii (?) Very rare.

P. Rouxii (?) D'Orb. Rare.

Solarium ornqtum. Rare.

Dentalium elliptium. Rather common.

Lamellibranchiata-

Ostrea vesicularis, Lam. Very common.

O. frons. Common.

O. macroptera. Very Rare.

Exogyra. sp. Very rare.

Plicatula sigillina. Very common.

P. pectinoides var. inflata. Sow. Common.

Spondylus truncatus. Rather rare.

Nucula simplex. Very rare.
perforated.

Inoceramus. Rare.

CRUSTACEA-

Hoploparia -

Fragments. Very rare.

ANNELIDA-

Serpula. Rather
common.

ECHINIDERMATA-

Spines. Rather rare.

COELENTERATA

Smilotrochus
elongatus. (Duncan)
Rare.

PROTOZOA-

Ventriculites.
Chenendopora.
rather common.

Parkeria. Rather rare.

DRIFT WOOD,

Radiolites Mortoni. Rare.

Taking this collection as affording a fair representation of the fauna of the Upper Greensand in this locality, and comparing it with the collection in the Woodward Museum at Cambridge, the almost entire absence of Echini (except the spines), the great rarity of Crustacea, the general absence of di-myrarian Lamellibranchiata, gasteropoda (except Pleurotomaria and Solarium, Dentalium) and Nautilus, and the commonness of Belemnites, are perhaps worthy of note. The specimens are also much less perfect than at Cambridge, and are generally very badly preserved."

(Fordham, H. F.G.S. (1866), 'On a Collection of Fossils from the Upper Greensand, of Morden, Cambridgeshire.' Proc. Geol. Assoc. Vol. IV)

By the end of 1867 Guilden Morden's vicar had realised that, with coprolite workings in fields adjoining his glebe, the seam extended under his land. He allowed Mr Merry, a local farmer, to work them but a formal agreement was never drawn up and then Merry died. Mr Hale Wortham, acting for the vicar, arranged to have the land surveyed. by Clement Francis. (CCRO. Francis Bill Books, December 23rd 1867,p.369) Jesus College, who had the advowson of the church, consented to having them raised. On April 15th 1868, James Ind Headley, the Cambridge iron founder, was given an agreement by the vicar to work twelve acres of the glebe in Little Green. A sketch map can be seen in the illustrations. The college had valued the coprolites at £80 per acre but, as prices were up to £2.50 a ton that year, Headley was prepared to pay £100 per acre for land which previously had an agricultural rent of only £18 per annum. Clearly, the prospect of a relative fortune would not have been lost on the vicar and the college.

The workings were shown on the first geological map of the area, seen in the illustrations. They were about one and a half miles north of the village on both sides of the road near North Brook Farm. (1" Geol. 46NE) They were around a low ridge of chalk marl that overlay the nodule bed. The best documentation for these working that has emerged has been from St. John's and Jesus College's archives. Other landowners would have given leases to either their tenant farmers or outside contractors but their records, as yet, have not come to light.

The diggings in Hinxworth gradually spread northwards towards Dunton Lodge Farm and in 1868 the owner, maybe Ernest Fordham, arranged to have them raised. The farm was tenanted by Simeon Lee and Jonas Carver. Whether their farm labourers were involved in the work is uncertain but the owner wanted to sell it with the mining rights and receive a considerably better price than just as an agricultural estate. The Dunton Estate was put up for sale in July that year and the sale particulars pointed out that

"*Dunton Lodge Farm contains VALUABLE BEDS OF COPROLITES, which are being worked by the owner. There are also large Deposits on the Church Farm and some on Millow Bury."*

(BCRO. WG.2359)

Subsequent evidence shows that Lawes had either bought the estate or won a coprolite lease from the purchaser. A few months later, Lawes' Hitchin-based surveyor, George Beaver, noted in his diary, *"On the 5th October 1868 I am coprolite surveying at Dunton Lodge Farm near Biggleswade for J. B. Lawes."* By November he reported that, *"Coprolite work in full swing"* and in the following year he noted that *"All 1869 J.B. Lawes' people very busy in diggings which take up a great deal of my time."* (Hitchin Museum, G. Beaver's diaries, pp.86a,87a.)

One by-product of the diggings was gravel. Unwanted by the manure manufacturers it had to be separated from the coprolites and sold for use on drives, paths or on improving roads. Many roads were damaged by coprolite traffic. Wallis' foreman, Abraham Pearman, sold 100 tons to the Surveyor of the Highways without permission from the college bursar. Concerned about such impropriety, St. John's College bursar, Mr Reyner ,visited the workings but, on seeing great heaps of sifted gravel that had been brought up by the workmen, he conceded that its sale should go ahead - but for the benefit of the college. In May, David Greig, of the Arrington and Caxton Highways Board in Melbourn, wrote to Reyner offering a shilling a ton (£0.05) per cubic yard of gravel.

"The getting of it will be considerable therefore cannot give more and do hope that you take into consideration the excessive traffic on these roads caused by the digging of coprolites and that you will accede to the above proposals."

(St. John's Mun. Box. Steeple Morden)

Especially in wet weather the wheels of tumbrils laden with

fossils trundling the four and a half miles down to Odsey and Ashwell station caused considerable damage to the roads. There was plenty of money to be made by the carters. (O'Connor, B. (1999), 'The Dinosaurs on Bassingbourn Fen', Bernard O'Connor, Gamlingay)

The extra income from both the coprolite and the gravel would have been welcome for any landowner, especially since farm rents were still only between twenty and thirty shillings (£1.00 - £1.50) per acre at this time. St. John's 209a.1r.9p. Kirkby Manor Farm in Ashwell was valued in July 1865 at £386 with a rental of only twenty-seven shillings (£1.35) an acre.

In November 1869 Rev. Pigott, the rector of Abington Pigotts, having discovered the coprolites on part of the arable field belonging to his glebe, wrote to the Ecclesiastical Commissioners, *"I am desirous of disposing of the so called mineral and investing the money for the benefit of the living."* However, administration took time then as it does today and it was not until July the next year before the Commissioners drew up a lease. Interestingly it was Colchester who won the contract. He was allowed to raise them from 5a.3r.15p of the 22a.0r.7p. glebe at £100 per acre over a period of three years. The rector later admitted, *"an additional endowment of almost £600 derived from royalties from coprolites between 1869 and 1871."* The dividends from which must have been a very welcome addition to church funds. (VCH. 'Cambs.' pp.8-9; London Church Comm.files, 41857. Abington in the Clay)

Following the end of the Franco-Prussian War in 1870 there was a period of relative peace and stability across Europe. Great Britain's population continued to increase which intensified farmers' fertiliser requirements to meet the increased demand for food. The importance of the coprolites in the export trade should not be undervalued and neither should their contribution to the French wine industry! Superphosphate was sold in France as a vital fertiliser when their vineyards had been devastated by "phylloxera," a bug which attacked the roots of the vine. New stock had to be imported from Californian vineyards which had themselves been planted with French vines. Viticulturalists assisted its early growth with the application of the best fertiliser on the market. (Campling, H. Beds. Times September 1939; Yates, R. "History of Potton," unpublished papers, p.44) Coprolite prices increased 20% in two year to £3.00 a ton in 1870.

This was evidenced in 1871 when Wallis' workmen had succeeded in digging 3a.0r.16p over the winter. *"We have been rapidly pushing them on as our trade is better."* In September his manager, Abraham Pearman, who was living in one of the cottages at North Brook End, was keen to extract the remaining coprolites. However, some old buildings stood over the deposit in front of a small row of cottages. Wallis approached Mr Reyner for permission *"as the coprolites under the garden are good and at about 8' to 8'6" depth instead of 13' to 13'6" as in the field."* He also suggested that buildings should be demolished and replaced once the coprolite had been worked. The college agreed. He suggested that he would work them to within sixty poles or so of the cottages and to have the whole operation finished in six or eight weeks. The college had plans drawn up for the erection of new accommodation *"comprising a potatoe and coal place for each cottage with an oven in common."* The costs were to be met from their coprolite fund. Perhaps understandably, the cottagers were happy enough with the compensation; their major concern was that they had somewhere to plant their vegetables. The college arranged for a survey to be done which revealed that his men had dug 5a.2r.27p., not including the cottage garden, so the Bursar gave permission on the following terms:-

1. You do not approach the cottage walls nearer than say 10 feet.
2. That in consideration of the coprolites being comparatively near the surface in the garden the compensation to the college be increased from £80 to £100.

81

> 3. That the cottagers be allowed by you every facility for growing potatoes on the land already dug but not filled up.
>
> (St. John's Mun. Box. Steeple Morden)

Wallis' men had dug over 1a.2r.27p. of the garden by August, paying the college £153 10s.0d. When they had completed the work, St. John's had realised £387, the value of a small estate and probably more than enough to pay for the new buildings.

According to the 1871 census the coprolite diggings were claimed as halting the emigration from the countryside to the towns. The populations of Abington Pigotts, Bassingbourn, Croydon, Kneesworth, Litlington, Guilden Morden, Steeple Morden and Shingay-cum-Wendy increased by 874. Nearly four hundred men and boys were employed in these parishes. Over the 1860s Guilden Morden's population increased 17% to 1059. As seventy-two men and boys were described as engaged in the work it must have been linked with the diggings. (Cambridge Village Book, 1989, p.90) As this number was far more than would have been needed on Wallis' small field there must have been other local workings. The number of dwellings in the village had doubled to over 200 which, according to the Victoria County History, was related to the growing affluence of the inhabitants. (VCH. 'Cambs.', vol.8 p.112.) There were three gravel diggers and fifty-four fossil diggers. 30-year old William Parish was the "*Fossil Foreman*" living on Hay Street. Also involved were a fossil washer, three fossil carters and three engine drivers who may well also have been employed hauling truckloads of fossils over the fields to the washmill. Here there were two millers, Edward Jarman and William Whitehead, a "*labourer in mill*" and a miller's carter. The average age was twenty-nine and ranged from sixty-five to fourteen. Considering that only ninety-six men were working on the farms, it shows the importance of the diggings for the village economy. (CCRO. RG 10/1359; Rep.Com.Univ. Income.p.379.) Table I in the appendix shows how it was predominantly older man's work. As in most of the coprolite villages, the majority of those employed were locals with only a few born outside the parish. Table II shows their home locations.

Steeple Morden's population increased 11.5% over the decade to 1018 with sixty-nine men and boys employed in the diggings. There were three coprolite foremen. 33-year old John Haylock lived on Pound Green, 44-year old William Izzard lived on the High Street and 29-year old James Badwell lived in the "Fossil Hut near "Dabs knole," with his wife and six children! He came from Swaffham, another parish on the "coprolite belt" which suggests he was attracted here by the works. 80% of the diggers were born in the parish and 16% came from nearby parishes. The eldest was 58 and the youngest was 12 and, although there was a majority of men in their early twenties, the average age was 29.5, showing that it was the older men that dominated the work. This was a similar pattern as in other parishes on the coprolite belt but the age structure can be seen more clearly on Table III. Other associated occupations were a well borer, two engine drivers and a "fossil carter." Their home locations can be seen on Table IV.

Litlington's decline in population was reversed with a 10% increase of seventy-five to 768. Of the 400 males 17% were agricultural workers and 13% were involved in the coprolite business. George Sharp, aged 35, was the *Foreman of the Fossil Works*" and there were fifty-one coprolite diggers. John Cole was the eldest at 65 and Walter Smith, aged 9, the youngest. He ought to have been at school! The average age was 30.4. There were also seven lodgers who were all from outside the area but with 71% born locally and 55% of them married it was generally local employment for the older men. There were twenty-seven involved in Hinxworth, seven in Abington Pigotts and four in Ashwell but surprisingly none across the stream in Dunton or Eyeworth. (CCRO. 1871 census; VCH. 'Cambs.', vol. 8. pp.54,61; Also see O'Connor, B. 'The Ashwell Fossil Diggings', Bernard O'Connor, Gamlingay)

Not long after the census was taken there was an event which must have occasioned an even greater influx of diggers into the area. Wages had begun to rise in many sections of employment and when prices for Cambridgeshire coprolite rose to £3.80 a ton the profitability of the coprolite business must have prompted some labourers to take industrial action.

> "*ASHWELL = We understand there has been a strike at the coprolite works in this neighbourhood and that now labourers are in demand at the increased rate of wages. It is an opportunity for many to improve their position.*"
>
> (Potton Journal, 17th June 1871)

This was the only documented case of its kind on the coprolite belt but in the fens there were cases of "Unionism" amongst the diggers. It is worth noting that the Cambridge Chronicle and Royston Crow made no mention of the strike. It would not have been the done thing when its owners and advertisers were probably local capitalists.

In April that year, Rev. Wilson, the vicar of Guilden Morden, acknowledged in correspondence with the Church Commissioners that, "*the sum of £820 had accrued to the living through the digging of coprolites on the glebe during the year just elapsed (1871).*" This brought on a large-scale investigation as to his having illegally allowed the coprolites to be raised. In his explanatory letter he revealed what happened.

Guilden Morden,
Royston,
25th April 1872
File No.46,166

Sir,

In reply to your communication dated 23rd April, I beg to say that the coprolites on the glebe were dug in perfect ignorance of the Acts of Parliament which require the consent of the Ecclesiastical Commissioners. The case stands thus. A few months after my appointment to this

Living in November 1867, knowing that there were coprolites on this portion of the glebe, I put the matter into the hands of a solicitor at Cambridge, with the consent of the patrons, instructing him to draw up a lease between Mr J. I. Headly and myself. I should say that the late vicar, just prior to his death had commenced to work them without any lease and, I believe, without the consent of the Patrons. It therefore appears that the Solicitors were in ignorance when they drew up the Deed, that the Consent of the Ecclesiastical Commissioners was requisite to dig coprolites. The Patrons too, must be unaware of the clause which requires that monies so obtained shall be invested by the Commissioners. The money which has accrued to the Living is invested by them; they being the Trustees. Of course, I much regret to find a step has been taken which is illegal, and I wish to say that I shall be in London between April 30 and May 4 and shall be glad to give any explanation at the Office respecting this matter and will bring the lease with me,

      I am, Sir
      Yours faithfully,
         J. N. Wilson.
(CCRO. Church Comm. files, Guilden Morden,1984)

The bursar of Jesus College had agreed to invest the money in consols for the benefit of the vicar and, if there was "no legal obstacle," use the money to build a "Vicarage House." The Commissioners, however, asked for the dividends from the investments and they "agreed" to become trustees of a new fund which had amounted to £824.1s.5d. by 1873. The terms of their agreements would not allow a new building to be constructed so they compromised, willing to enlarge and improve the lath and plaster, seven feet high vicarage which Rev. Wilson had described as *"small, ill-built and unfit for habitation."* In 1874 a large, grey-brick wing was added, paid for out of the royalties of coprolites. (VCH. 'Cambs.' p.108)

In 1872 the financial success of the manure manufacturers led a group of businessmen to suggest a take over of Lawes' Manure Company. One of them was William Colchester. The profits from his patent, his manure business and coprolite contracts made him an extremely wealthy man - a typical Victorian entrepreneur. From 1869 to 1872 his company had a growth rate of 10%. (Valence House Museum, Dagenham, (VHM), Lawes Chemical Manure Co. Minute Books 16th November 1880) After 30 years in the business he eventually agreed to sell up. On 1st July 1872 he sold his *"valuable and extensive business"* for £300,000, the present day equivalent of about £9 million! The new directors could see a potential expansion of the manure trade with the development of overseas phosphate exploration. For trade reasons they kept the name Lawes Chemical Manure Company and took over all his existing coprolite leases. This ensured the continuation of his local contracts.

By the autumn of 1872 Wallis was ready to move on. He wrote to Reyner at St. John's about his workings at Steeple Morden.

> *"We have finished at Morden with the exception of the mound where we washed the coprolites and one or two small pieces that my foreman does not consider sufficiently dry to put the mound on to."*

(St. John's Mun. Box. Steeple Morden)

The surveyor's map in the illustrations shows the men had dug 6a.3r.31p. He therefore had paid £589 to the college. (SJC Archives SB21.162 coprolite papers) As royalties had risen by this time to over £100 per acre, the prosperity of those involved naturally attracted the attention of William Warboys, the local Income Tax assessor. He wrote to Reyner in August 1872 asking how much the college had realised for the purpose of assessing the tax but Reyner argued that, only receiving royalties, it ought to be Wallis who was the one to be taxed. He sent him form 11B, Schedule D. Warboys wrote back informing him that, *"all parties who have sold any coprolite land are charged the royalty they receive from the purchaser during the year."* Deciding not to implicate the college in financial wrangling, the next day he sent a cheque for £42 6s. 0d. being 20% of the Property Tax. (St. John's Mun. Box. Steeple Morden; Rep. Univ. Income, St. John's College 1871)

All the concern about how much money the parish, the colleges and landowners could realise from having the land worked hid the fact that the diggings were still considered a social problem. The Methodists and the Coprolite Visiting Societies must have had some influence but Thomas Darcy, the curate of Shingay-cum-Wendy provided a measure of their success in his 1873 report to the Bishop of Ely.

"The great hindrance (to your ministerial success) is the proximity of coprolite works, as those gathered there are the worst from all parishes and the natural tendency of this is bad in all ways. The Coprolite works have added Public Houses (and) ... have increased the demand and the remuneration for labour and have decreased education. Labourers have the making but Nick keeps them in poverty. If the employers of labour interested themselves personally in the moral well-being of their workmen, then we could do very well in this parish."

(CUL.EDR.C3/25)

In early summer 1873, following the expiry of the 21-year lease of Jesus College Farm the bursar arranged for a survey. Charles Bidwell reported that

"Nos. 1 - 12, about 40 acres, contain coprolites. Some of the adjoining land has been dug and they would readily let at a high price per acre as they are within easy distance of the surface and adjoining good roads."

(CCRO. Bidwell 28 p.256)

James Hunt, the new tenant, took over the farm and Edward Long was asked to undertake an extensive survey. His sketch map can be seen in the illustrations. It shows that the Earl of Hardwick and Mr Lilley owned the neighbouring fields. As the geological map shows workings across this area they too must have made a good profit from having the coprolites dug. It was not until April 1877, however, that the bursar was ready to do anything about College Farm. He had previously been approached by Luke Griffin, a Cambridge coprolite merchant, who managed a number of works for the Lawes Artificial Manure Company.

> *"12 Brunswick Place,*
> *Cambridge.*
>
> *Jesus College,*
> *Dear Mr.Corrie,*
> *I made some time ago a personal application on behalf of Mr J.B. Lawes of 29 Mincing Lane, London about some land containing coprolites at Morden in the occupation of Mr Hunt. At that time I think you were given to believe there was only a small portion which contained coprolites. From further enquiries I believe there are from 25 - 30 acres. Mr Lawes is quite willing to pay £1,000 - £1,200 and further sums as the work advances...*
> *Luke Griffin"*
> (Jesus College Mun. Steeple Morden)

Lawes and the new company had been working the coprolites in Ashwell, Hinxworth, Astwick, Dunton and many of the villages westwards towards Shitlington, as it was then known. Despite twenty years of the diggings there were still extensive deposits available - but at much lower depths. Obviously the most accessible seams had been exploited first. William Colchester's brother, Edward, had earlier moved into in Down Hall Farm to supervise extensive workings in Abington Pigotts and Bassingbourn and Lawes' company clearly wanted to maintain their interests in the area. However, their offer of only £40 per acre was far below the current royalties. Presumably aware of this, Edward Colchester made an offer of £100 an acre, one which the college couldn't really refuse. Jesus College's surveyor reported to Rev. Corrie, hinting that there may well have been problems over other similar agreements in the past.

"The price, upon seeing some of the coprolites raised, I think is a very fair one - and the terms such as to avoid disputes... My own experience and recent observations made upon works carried on by various Raisers have proved that the yield or number of tons per acre in this district as in nearly all fleet work, is much smaller in comparison with that of Central Cambridgeshire, as well as the quality being inferior. The Royalty in no case approaching that of the latter district..."

	Quantity
Approx. quantity	
	containing cops.
11,12 Honey Hill	*27.3.11*
	5.2. 0
16 Nut Grove Close	*4.3.38*
	4.3.38
17,18 Great Close, Calves Pightle	
19,20 Hog yard, Cottages & buildings	*22.1.37*
	21.0. 0
55.	*1. 6. 3*
	1.1.38

(Jesus College, Mun. Steeple Morden)

The bursar was advised that *"The offer of digging these portions (17 and 19) for coprolites presenting a very favourable opportunity for so doing if properly conducted."* The college agreed and in October 1877, Rev. Corrie, signed an agreement allowing Edward Colchester to raise them at the same £100 an acre Wallis had paid in 1872.

Another coprolite contractor, Henry Coningsby of Melbourn, had won an agreement with Herbert Fordham to work his fields in Guilden Morden. When he first started is unknown but he had been working the coprolites in Potton since 1866. In August 1873 he had his coprolite plant valued. The surveyor's notebook indicated that at least three coprolite mills were in operation. Although part of the plant was retained by Fordham, the sale realised £109 6s.0d. (CCRO. 296B485 pp.41-44) This was not the end of the diggings however, or of Coningsby's involvement. Landlords were still keen to realise the best price for their land. Even in 1876, one of the absentee landlords, tried to sell "coprolite" land.

"*Coprolites. Seven acres of coprolites at Guilden Morden, Cambs. to be sold by private treaty. The bed is good, and is situate within an easy distance of the Ashwell and Royston stations, on the G.N.R. - For particulars and orders to bore apply to Messrs. Norris and Ashwell, Solicitors, St. Leonard's-on-Sea, Sussex.*"

(CC, 6th May,1876)

No evidence has emerged as to who might have bought it or whether it was worked. Who the landowner was is also uncertain. The best-documented evidence has come from the college archives. Smaller landowners may well have engaged local solicitors and surveyors and their records have not been deposited in the Record Offices. Newspapers provide additional information. The Royston Crow reported at the end of 1876 that there were workings on Mr Sayle's field.

"*GUILDEN MORDEN. On Wednesday last a youth named Arthur Matthews, who resides in the village, was employed in the Coprolite Works in Mr Sayle's field. He unfortunately got too near the spindle of the engine and some portion of his dress was caught by it. He appears to have been dragged down to the ground and twisted round the spindle two or three times before the engine could be stopped. Upon being extricated he was found to be seriously injured, and when medical attendance was procured, it was found necessary to send him to the Cottage Hospital, Royston... It was found that he had a fracture of his right thigh and a serious lacerated wound to the left thigh. We hear he is as good as could possibly be expected; the wonder is he was not more seriously injured, and that he was not immediately killed."*

(RC, November 17th 1876)

In January 1878, one of the local coprolite diggers, Samuel Wenham, was sent for twenty-one days imprisonment with hard labour after he admitted assaulting and beating up another labourer before Christmas. (RC,11th Jan.1878) Whether he got his job back when he came out is unknown but probably unlikely if he had been working for Coningsby on Fordham's land. By the early summer these workings had finished and the auction of the coprolite plant was arranged. The details were also reported in the Crow.

"GUILDEN MORDEN, 2 miles from Ashwell Station, Instructed by Herbert Fordham Esq., the diggings being completed, to sell by auction, THE COPROLITE PLANT on Thurs. May 17th 1877 at 2 for 3 o'clock comprising two 8-Horse power portable engines in good condition by Harrison of Northampton and Burrel, A slub wheel, washing mill complete, 2 sets of harrows, 22 leather straps, a Water tank, 40-round ladder and tools, Timber framed engine house, stable and offices and 800 yards of iron tramway and sleepers."

(RC, April 27th, May 11th 1877)

The sale realised £147 2s.3d. and a considerable proportion was sold to other contractors and farmers like Griffin, Wallis, Masters, Howard and Coningsby. (CCRO. 296B945.6) Despite this closure, there is evidence that coprolite land was still being bought in the parish but, as shall be seen, the economics of the business were changing. There was another sale in June 1878 of North Brook End Farm. Its sale particulars revealed that lot 2, 2a.1r.8p., was *"believed to contain a bed of coprolites next to Pightle."* The whole estate was bought by the Ecclesiastical Commissioners for £4,500 but Frederick King of Royston paid them £170 for the coprolites. He had just taken over Fordham's Odsey Mill and was already supplying the Royston Farmers Manure Company. In the spring, when the work got under way, a considerable number of oak trees had to be felled and their roots raised in order to allow the fields to be worked. In the meantime James Hunt, the tenant farmer of Jesus College Farm, died and John Hunt, probably his son, took over the 174a.0r.3p. Farm and Homestead paying the sum of £284 1s. 3d. As shall be seen, it was not a good investment!

Colchester made a further agreement with Jesus College for a further 7a.3r.2p. so that by summer 1878 he had twenty-five acres in his occupation. By February 1879 he had dug 5a.1r.9p. using two mills, one horse-operated and the other steam driven. Later, he made another request to get the coprolites from under the gardens on Jesus College Farm. Hunt was contacted with the request that he "*be pleased to oblige the College by giving up the two cottages from Michaelmas last by their deducting the rent of the same.*" (Jesus College, Mun. Steeple Morden)

The continued availability of deposits encouraged King to purchase 2a.1r.8p in North Brooke End, a plot adjacent to Jesus College land "*believed to contain coprolites*". He only paid £170. This was much cheaper than a few years earlier. Maybe he thought it was a bargain? He seemed ignorant of the changing fortune of the coprolite market. (CCRO. 296B949.4; RC 29th May 1885)

The latter half of the 1870s was dominated by bad weather. There were four consecutive years of heavy rain which ruined crops and reduced harvests. In the summer of 1877 there was a severe electrical storm which caused lightning fires in Ashwell and Orwell. Four lambs were killed in Arrington and

"*during the heavy thunderstorm that visited this neighbourhood on Wednesday afternoon, a horse belonging to Mr Johnson, Coprolite Merchant, was killed, the tree beneath which it was standing being struck by lightning."*

(RC, 17th August 1877)

Maybe the stress was telling as in spring the following year, Mr Morgan was charged with ill treating a horse and making it work when it was ill. He was fined thirty-three shillings (£1.65), about two week's wages for a fossil digger. This was only sixpence (£0.025) less than one of the diggers in Bassingbourn was charged for assaulting another labourer! (RC,22nd Feb.1878)

The bad weather seriously affected farmers. Their economic problems were exacerbated by the then Tory government's introduction of Free Trade. This allowed entrepreneurs to capitalise on the newly developed refrigerated shipping and import vast quantities of cheap meat and grain surpluses from the American Prairies and South American Pampas into Great Britain. Home prices plummeted. Wheat prices fell to a half of what they were in the 1860s. Many farmers were forced out of business. Some were successful in arranging rent reductions of up to 30% but others were evicted. Many farms were untenanted and there was a knock on effect on local services. Trade fell and huge numbers of agricultural and other labourers were forced to accept lower wages or were laid off.

Edward Colchester, with his father's knowledge of the changing economic fortune of the diggings, wanted to scale down his operations and arranged the auction of some of his plant in Wendy. It was advertised in the Royston Crow.

To Coprolite raisers, machinists and others.
WENDY, CAMBS.
On Tuesday 31st July 1877 an extensive and valuable
COPROLITE PLANT
including a 10 Horse-power PORTABLE ENGINE (nearly

new) by Robey & Co., an 8 Horse-power Ditto by Ransomes and Sims (nearly new), both complete with Engine Cover, Tools, etc., about 40 tons of TRAMWAY METAL (in lots), 3 Washing Rings (for steam power) with 3/4 Inch Iron Bottoms, Spindles, Crown Wheels, Harrows, Grates,etc. (complete as fixed), Planks, Barrows, trucks, Bars, 2 Slurry Wheels, cast iron and Zinc pumps, 6 Engine Straps, 800 of Deal Boards, Seasoned Ash and Elm quarterings, cart shafts, and Planks, 4 Engine Sheds, Slurry Troughing, Water Tanks, Blacksmith's Tools, and a Steam Saw bench (by Sparks of Norwich), harness for 10 horses, 4 Scotch Carts, complete, also 5 POWERFUL CART HORSES, in good condition."

(Royston Crow 27th July,1877)

Examination of the papers at this time show considerable unrest in the area. Tensions in Steeple Morden were created when men were laid off. One instance was reported in November 1878 when David Hall, a local farmer, had just laid off labourers from his fossil pit. This was the first and only mention of his involvement. Many other small landowners probably had their own fossil pits. David Covington had gone for a beer when he was supposed to be at work but was seen. Hall fired him the next morning. In revenge Covington set alight to Hall's straw stack and, when caught, shouted, "Now take me - I'd have seven years for it; I'll never go into a coprolite pit any more." Moses Chamberlain, another coprolite digger from Bassingbourn, said he had met Covington in Sidney Wilmott's beerhouse where, although he did not go into details, he must have been aware of some grievance as he heard him say he was going to set it alight. "Prisoner had been in the fossil pit that week and had offered to sell his books."

Maybe the pressure of having a hard task master, the working conditions or some personal problem had arisen as Covington was reported to have added, "I don't mean to do any more stone digging." He was sent for trial. Whether he did do any more diggings in not known. Grievance seemed to be quite widespread in Steeple Morden as there were at least three more cases of incendiarism in the village over that Christmas. (RC, 13th November,1878) Insight into the revival of the conflict between farmers and labourers was provided by the following song. It came from a newspaper cutting kept in Rev. Pigotts notes on the diggings.

COPROLITE DIGGING FOREVER

SUCCESS TO THE FOSSIL DIGGERS!

Come listen you farmers to what I do say,
We Coprolite diggers now can have fair play,
You once did us grind down, but now its our turn,
As we can get work and farm labour spurn!
We are jolly young fellows, that do not work fear,
We can work at the fossils, have a pot of good beer
With our spade and pickaxe we've no work to seek
We won't work for farmers for ten bob a week.

So good luck to all labourers wherever they may be,
The Coprolite diggers I mean for to say; .
Success to all men that can use the spade,
He's quite as well off as a man at his trade.

Remember old farmer you once had your way,
Of crushing poor labourers and make them obey,
But now we have plenty of work for to do,
So go to the d----l and all the fine crew; .
Your sons & daughters with all their fine clothes
At the Coprolite diggers don't turn up your nose,
Remember t'was through us you have what you've got,
But still for all that you're a covetous lot.

But Willie and Johnny must follow their plough,
And Betty and Polly must go milk the cows; .
They must pull off their hoops and look to their dairy,
And not go a flirting with Tommy and Jerry; .

The farmer's sons too have got tears in their eyes,
For they'll have to work hard, and that is no lies,
Since Coprolite digging is now all the go,
They'll get no stone diggers to follow a plough.

There's many a man you'll say it's no lie,
That will make the poor farmers to sigh and to cry,
Thro' leaving their work when they're real good men,
But what is the use when you've nothing to spend; .
For the coprolite digging it now is alive,
They are sure to prosper which makes men to thrive,
You farmers are nothing but covetous elves,
You never spend anything, but want all for yourselves.

I've been to some works in famed Coldham's Lane,
And I've heard it repeated again and again,
That Poss will get married to red-headed Sall,
And I hope she will make him a very good pal; .
There's Tifey he loves a drop of good beer,
And Hello he is not behind, never fear,
There's Pegg too he's fond of a little wee drop,
And Blinkee he keeps the swankey beer shop.

There's no harm in what I'm going to say,
But if you should meet them by night or by day,
They will ask you a question and often repeat,
Hello! old fellow, how is your poor feet?
Where are you going on Sunday? they say,
Or anything else that comes in their way;
But still I respect them, they are hard working men,
And this is the reason I took up my pen.

So now I conclude with good luck to you all,
The lads and the men, the great and the small,
you are jolly good fellows wherever you be,
And where you got one bob, I hope you'll get three.

(Original in possession of the Sclaters, Abington Pigotts)

The coprolite contractors suffered too during this period. Increased rainfall made the work in the pits dangerous. In Ashwell Museum one can see the "creepers", iron grips that the diggers fastened round the sole of the boot to stop them from slipping in wet mud. Also on display are iron insteps that stopped the spade from wearing away the boots. The rain also increased pumping costs with the additional water and made it difficult to properly dry out the slurry. On top of this, newly discovered rock phosphate from Charleston, South Carolina, had started to be shipped into British ports in the early-1870s. In 1876 coprolite production was 258,150 tons. The following year it dropped to 69,006 tons whilst 170,000 tons of American phosphate was imported with a value of £500,000. These rock phosphates were very similar in nature to the East Anglian coprolites but, in typical American fashion, they were on a far greater scale and variety. The Charleston News and Courier of 1880 reported that

"These deposits consist of nodules of phosphate of lime, thickly interspersed with the huge bones and teeth of antediluvian mammalian and marine mammoths of stupendous and gigantic proportions; the chrysonicocrisides, ichthyosauri, hadrosauri, stupendous giant baboons, prodigious mammoth gorillas, lizards 33 feet long, and other huge graminovorous and carnivorous quadrupeds; also the squaladons, phocodons, dinotherinons, and members of the ichthaurian, saurian and cetacean families, whales 500 feet long, sharks 200 feet long, briny leviathons, voracious marine vultures and other monster, rapacious denizens of the mighty deep - land and water animals lying in the same bed. These wonderful and awe-inspiring skeleton remains, styled by Professor Agassiz "the greatest cemetery in the world," constitute by far the most valuable fertiliser known to man since the exhaustion of the Peruvian guano deposits; and are an inexhaustible source of wealth to the State

and people of South Carolina, and thence to the whole world."

(Charleston News and Courier, Industrial Issue, (1880))

It was a thick seam at shallow depths around the estuary mouth and the companies working it employed cheap Black labour to dig it out. It had a higher quality phosphate content than the British coprolite and even with transport costs it sold in Great Britain at much cheaper rates. Many coastal manure companies reduced their purchases of local coprolites with the result that prices dropped an average of 20% to £2.40 a ton. Inland companies, as shall be seen, maintained their demand but at much lower prices. This made many operations uneconomic. In many parishes pits were abandoned. In the summer months they made good swimming pools. Sheds were locked and plant and machinery left to rust. Coprolite contractors asked to be allowed reductions of their leases. Some landowners agreed but others refused and forced them to continue with the terms of their agreement and forcing them into bankruptcy. Coprolite labourers joined the many other unemployed in the area. Production fell to 30,500 tons in 1880. The Agricultural Depression had set in.

Manure manufacturers suffered too. With the bad weather and foreign competition farmers were not willing to buy fertilisers to grow food that they could not sell. The prices of "super" fell to as low as five pounds ten shillings (£5.50) a ton. This downward spiral in trade came full circle when the manure manufacturers stopped their purchases of the overseas phosphates. There was no market for "super". The decline in the industry's fortune was varied. Aware of the industry's changing fortune, many contractors pulled out of uneconomic ventures and concentrated in parishes where there were still seams worth exploiting. As in farming, wages were reduced which meant many of the young, single men looked for work elsewhere.

Many manure manufacturers, in intense competition with each other, lowered prices to increase their share of the market.

Some reverted to the early practice of adulterating the superphosphate, giving the industry a bad name. It is worth noting that British farmers' reduced demand for "super" caused almost identical problems for the American suppliers as those experienced by the British coprolite contractors. The South Carolina Ministry of Agriculture described the problem in early 1880 as being

"...a very general and widespread depression prevailing in the production of river rock. As is generally known, the great bulk of this rock is shipped to foreign countries. The short crops, and general agricultural distress which has for some years past spread over the whole of Europe, had most seriously affected the capacity of the farmer to purchase and pay for fertilisers, and consequently diminished to a very large degree the demand for the Carolina rock. Thus not only was the market lost, to a great extent, but the prices at which the rock could be sold were very greatly diminished. In consequence of this, river mining became unprofitable. A large number of the smaller companies ceased work entirely, and even the larger ones were compelled very greatly to curtail their operations and to continue with a much reduced force and at great loss."

('First Annual Report of the Commissioner of Agriculture of the State of South Carolina.' Walker, Evans & Cogswell, Charleston, (1880), pp.11-12.)

With American supplies all but halted in 1880 there was a revival in demand for coprolite, albeit at lower prices. Inland manufacturers, like Fordhams of Odsey, Birds of Duxford, Colchester and Ball of Burwell had many directors and shareholders on their boards who still had coprolite land. Joseph Nunn, the chairman of and the Farmers Manure Company of Royston, had an extensive deposit on his Bassingbourn Farm. The cost of freighting in the new phosphates was high and there was a policy of wanting to ensure a continuing business for some of their customers who might otherwise have been in financial difficulties. As a result some parishes maintained their coprolite industry during this difficult period.

According to the 1881 census the populations of Abington Pigotts, Bassingbourn, Croydon, Kneesworth, Litlington, Guilden Morden, Steeple Morden and Shingay-cum-Wendy fell by 356 yet there were still over two hundred men and boys involved. This was despite significant out-migration of the economically active age group. Guilden Morden's population dropped 9% over the decade to 959 yet the census revealed that there were fifty-three employed. This was one of the largest numbers on the coprolite belt after Barrington with 120, Bassingbourn with 75 and Orwell with 58. It was still a very much local occupation with 71.1% born in the parish, most of the rest were born in nearby parishes. The eldest was 64 and the youngest 15. Table I shows that there was a large group of teenagers at work but with the average age of 30.1.

Steeple Morden's population fell by 13% to 981. There were thirty-one still employed in the diggings, less than half the 1871 figure. There was no one recorded as "foreman" and out of the sixty-nine involved a decade earlier, surprisingly there were only three still working, Thomas Knott aged 39, William Ball, 45 and Samuel Wenham, 36. The average age was 26.8 with the eldest 45 and the youngest 12 but it is noticeable how much the 26 - 30 age group had declined. As only 58% were born locally and many were from other coprolite villages it suggests that a number had moved into the village to continue the work when it had finished in their parishes. The bulk of those employed earlier must have either gone back to farm or other work or left the area to find work in the towns.

There had been a 12% drop in Litlington to 674 yet there were fourteen still employed. Two men were portable engine drivers, who may well have been looking after the fossil mills or pumps at the diggings. There were twenty-eight in Bassingbourn and six in Abington Pigotts. The workings must have ceased in Hinxworth,

Ashwell and Dunton as there was no mention of anyone involved in the industry.

Montagu Fordham, another of the Fordham dynasty, was concerned about the numbers of young men who were leaving the area and had the results of his survey published in the Royston Crow.

since	1881 population (estimated)	No.Left between 1871-1881	No. left 1881
Guilden Morden	959	145	110
Steeple Morden	981	144	112

He claimed that many people blamed the large landowners and occupiers but he felt there were a large number of other factors which were responsible for the emigration. He claimed that improved agriculture and other machines had reduced labour and previously every farm used to have a malt house where their own and other's barley was malted. All agricultural implements used to be made locally but were now bought from large makers in towns. 6,000 quarters of corn used to be threshed by hand but now the chaff was cut and tied by machinery. Road materials used to be dug in the parish but now granite chippings were brought in from distant counties. There were eight to ten sawyers, many wheelwrights, carpenters and blacksmiths who made doors, gates and window frames which are now bought ready made and only fixed by the village carpenter. Spinning wheels were replaced by handlooms. Arable land had reverted to pasture as a result of foreign imports and labour had been attracted to the town by higher wages. Peasant proprietors found it impossible to rear profitable beef or mutton and they could not compete with the larger farmers for cereals. Local soils could not compete with the market gardening soils of Bedfordshire and Surrey. Fruit and vegetables were abundant here but the poorest lands that had been brought into production were going back to waste. Despite all this argument he went on to say that

"Our population does not care to emigrate - present wages, out-relief and various doles mean that life is pleasanter here for them than in any country in the world."

(RC, 28th August 1885)

Over the early-1880s there is no evidence that the diggings had restarted in the Mordens. The closure of the Parish reading room in 1884 with only twenty subscribers was linked to the demise of the diggings. (RC, 21st March 1884) There was no further mention of the coprolites until June 1888, following the death of Miss Horn. Her 134-acre Lodge Farm was auctioned and the sale particulars stated that the land was *"Old Pasture and Arable and containing VALUABLE BEDS OF COPROLITES."* (RC 15th April, 25th May 1888) James Sale was the tenant farmer at an annual rent of £182 per annum. After its sale the Royston Crow noted that,

"...it was stated that the land was believed to contain valuable beds of coprolites - for this reason the bidding commenced at £1,500 and eventually reached £2,700 at which price it was purchased by Mr J. Clear Wilkerson."

(Ibid. 29th June 1888)

Clear Wilkerson may well have been related to Henry Wilkerson who had extensive coprolite workings in Ashwell. (O'Connor, B. (1999), 'The Ashwell Fossil Diggings', Bernard O'Connor, Gamlingay) Perhaps he restarted the diggings selling it cheaply to Royston and Odsey? "Super" was being sold there as low as fifty shillings (£2.50) a ton in 1885, more than 60% less than when it was first on sale. Maybe Wilkerson's purchase stimulated further interest as a number of other local farms were auctioned shortly afterwards, including fifty acres of Thomas Parker's Dew Mead Farm. After several advertisements in the press, the advert was altered to state that *"a portion is believed to contain VALUABLE BEDS OF COPROLITES."* Whether this helped to sell it is not known but J.G. Russel paid £1,200 for it. (RC, 21st

June,12th July,1889) It seems very likely that both Wilkerson and Russel resumed the work.

In the early-1880s another extractive industry developed utilising the chalk marl in southwest Cambridgeshire. There were large-scale cement workings in Barrington and William Colchester ventured into the business in the Harston area. From Jesus College's accounts his men worked both cement and coprolites right through the 1890s finishing in 1905. (Kelly's Dir.1883, 1892,1896; Jesus Coll. Mun. estate papers 1877-86, Account books 1878 -1905)

The coal strike of 1890 had a severe effect on the profits of the coprolite contractors and cement manufacturers. The price of coal went up thereby further increasing costs. Many small-scale operations ceased operation which is evidenced in the 1891 census. The populations of Abington Pigotts, Bassingbourn, Croydon, Kneesworth, Litlington, Guilden Morden, Steeple Morden and Shingay-cum-Wendy fell by 593 over the decade. The Victoria County History gave the reason as being the lack of employment. (VCH. 'Cambs.', vol.8 p.139) Despite this exodus Edward Colchester was still described in Bassingbourn as a "*Coprolite Raiser employing 176 men*". According to the census, there were less than forty people in the area mentioned as involved. The others may well have been employed on his workings in other parishes on the coprolite belt. Guilden Morden's population had dropped a further 14.5% fall to 819 and there was no reference to any diggers. Steeple Morden's numbers fell 17% to 810 and only three men were engaged as "coprolite diggers". Litlington's population fell a further 15.7% to 568 and none were recorded there. Twenty-six were still employed in the diggings in Bassingbourn, six in Abington Pigotts but none in Ashwell, Hinxworth or Dunton. (CCRO. 1891 census)

There were still reserves worth exploiting in the 1890s as there was a record of work going on in Litlington as late as 1893 when Mr Russel's fields were being dug by Mr Colchester. He had a Coprolite works on Russel's land under the charge of

William Dellar. In March that year Dellar appeared at Arrington Petty Sessions charged with selling beer, probably Fordham's, without a licence. Mr Gibson, the Superior of Excise of Hitchin reported that

> "...The works were a long way off from a public house, and a cask or more of ale was obtained from a brewery (Fordham's? Ed.) and the men obtained the beer from Dellar, who deducted money from their wages at the week's end, according to the amount they had had. The beer was invoiced to Dellar, who admitted making a slight profit out of it. Profit, or no profit, however, that was of no importance, the sale of the beer was on Mr W. Russel's ground and that gentleman had been warned by both the excise officer living at Ashwell and by him, Mr Gibson, that it was illegal. George Collins of Bassingbourn employed by Mr Colchester at the diggings stated that if more was required then Russel sent on for it."

(RC 24th March 1893 p.6 col.1)

It was revealed that the beer was sold at 2d. (£0.01) a pint and the money was deducted from the men's pay on Friday. Dellar paid Russel for the beer having deducted two shillings (£0.10) in the pound commission. The prosecution felt there was not enough evidence to proceed against Russel or they would have done so. In the circumstances, the judge had to convict him but regretted doing so and instead of being fined the maximum £20 fine, Dellar was fined ten shillings (£0.50) with £1.10.6d. costs. The hope was expressed that Russel would help him pay! (RC,24th March,1893,p.6)

The industry's eventual demise was the result of a combination of factors. The major one was competition from cheaper, overseas rock phosphates, particularly from Charleston, South Carolina. Production restarted in 1881 and increased dramatically throughout the 1880s. Twenty-two contractors were working almost sixteen thousand acres (6,464 hectares) of phosphate land and capitalised on the cheap freight rates across the Atlantic. (Charleston Museum, South Carolina, unidentified publication in Major E.W. Willis' scrapbook, Marine and River Phosphate Mining Co.) By 1889 Algerian deposits had started to be exploited. In 1890 only 18,000 tons of coprolites were raised at the same time as 343,501 tons of phosphates were imported. By 1894 these had reached their peak of production at 380,289 at the same time as coprolite production fell to only 700 tons. By this time, even the inland manure factories relied on foreign supplies. Norway had started exporting its own superphosphate to Great Britain in the 1890s. As a result manufacturers' prices for coprolite dropped as low as nineteen shillings and sixpence (£0.97) per ton by 1892, several pounds lower than when at their peak. (VCM Lawes Chemical Manure Co. Minutes, 1892)

Local transport costs had risen. Railway companies had been charging contractors and manufacturers one shilling and two pence (£0.06) for a ton of coprolite or rock phosphate to be taken ten miles. With the introduction of the 1888 and 1892 Railway and Canal Acts the railway companies wanted price increases of over 100%. They wanted two shillings (£0.10) per ton for the same ten miles but if it was to a large town they wanted five shillings and sixpence (£0.28) per ton. A deputation from the Fertiliser Manufacturers Association petitioned Parliament to keep the transport price increases down, not only for British farmers but also for the nation's manure manufacturers. Rates were increased to two shillings and sixpence (£0.12). This led to reduced profits for the manure manufacturers, especially since the superphosphate, by this time, was selling at only £2.75 a ton. This was more than 50% lower than during the 1870s. (Fertiliser Manufacturers Association, (FMA.) Peterborough, Railway Rates 1888-94; Commercial matters 1890-98)

A further factor was the introduction in 1894 of the Quarries Act. This stipulated that if any pits were over twenty-five feet (6.14m.) deep, they had to conform to strict regulations as to safety requirements. By that time, most pits had to be at least twenty feet deep to extract the remaining deposits. The increased costs of such safety precautions were enough to deter those still in business.

Serious company losses were incurred which led eventually to mergers between manure companies. It is known that Mr Packard's and Mr Prentice's companies were taken over by Fisons of Ipswich but the late records of the smaller local companies, like the Cambridge Manure Company and the Royston Farmers Manure Company, unfortunately have failed to come to light. The local trade directories of that time confirm the industry's demise. When the industry was at its peak in 1876 there were twenty-three individual manure manufacturers, raisers and agents. The numbers dropped to only five in 1892. (Druce, D. (1881), 'Report on Cambs.' Royal Commission of Agriculture', p.365; Kelly's Post Office Directories, 1876,1892)

Where farmers or contractors had money available the pits were filled in and the ground levelled but many were left open. Even today water filled coprolite pits can still be seen. The last of the coprolite labourers were laid off and coupled with the decline in agriculture, Cambridgeshire became, for the time, one of the poorest counties in England. (Conybeare, E. (1897), 'History of Cambs.' p.268; Porter, E. (1971), op.cit.; OS. Cambridge Sheets 42/43 (1886)) There was a fall in farm rents, a decline in the amount of pasture and arable land and a change to vegetables and orchards. Along with the introduction of farm machinery, the closure of the coprolite works caused considerable out-migration and the demise of many trades. Many labourers joined the armed forces, some found alternative employment in agriculture and market gardening and others left the area to find employment in the urban centres. There is a report that some diggers went off to join the Klondyke Gold Rush in 1897. Public houses like "The Diggings" and "The Labour in Vain" closed and were converted to houses. This area returned to the quiet, peaceful atmosphere of previous generations with farming once again dominating the local economy.

There was a brief revival of the industry during the First World War. With the manure manufacturers total dependence on imported phosphate the German Navy targeted the merchant ships. The Fertiliser Manufacturers Association was asked to set up a commission to investigate the possibility of exploiting any remaining coprolite seams. Tests were done in Abington Pigotts but rev. Pigotts was against the reopening of the pits. Two very large-scale operations got underway in Grantchester and Trumpington in 1916. They provided valuable contracts to the operators but it is said that not one ton of coprolite left the site before the Armistice was signed in 1919. (O'Connor, B. (1998), 'The Dinosaurs on Coldham's Common', Bernard O'Connor, Gamlingay)

Another aspect which has helped which shed some light on the area's ancient history was the fact that in turning over hundreds of acres the diggers unearthed some interesting archaeological artefacts. The Cambridge solicitor, Clement Francis, aware of the value of these finds and the potential loss of revenue for the owners included a clause in his leases stipulating that "*all Coins, Armour, Bones, Fossils, Relics, Antiquaries & Curiosities which shall be discovered shall be the property of the landowner.*" (CCRO. Bendyshe Papers T14/1; CCRO. Francis Bill Books 1868 A-N pp.391-2) Iron Age pottery, Roman pewter plates, salt cellars and a scythe were found in pits in Abington Pigotts as well as prehistoric hut platforms. (Cambs. Arch. Record 03320/E) The vicar, Rev. Pigotts, had an article about these archaeological finds published in the 1886 Proceedings of the Cambridge Antiquarian Society, which also included details about the operations.

"*About eight chain less than half a mile nearly north of the parish church of Abington Pigotts there is undulating ground, in fact, a slight hill trending East and West, which has been turned over during the years 1879-84 for the purpose of extracting the coprolite under it... He observed the diggings and noted that a Roman settlement was uncovered. He called attention to holes used for domestic purposes. "I took special note of one of them on March 9th 1882 when I was of opinion that they were receptacles for funereal urns and I find in my notes that day, "The men employed in digging coprolite came across a hole three feet in diameter containing refuse etc. The hole went through a seam of coprolite; from the surface of the ground to the coprolite bed was 14 feet; ...The coprolite men used to take what they call a "fall" of 4ft. at a time, and from each fall in this particular trench did I get fragments of the bowl."*

(Pigott, Rev. G. (1886), 'Some account of the site of a Roman veteran's holding at Abington Pigotts,' Proceedings of the Cambridge Antiquarian Society. vi pp.309-12 46)

Close to Manor Farm was Bellus Hill, a low mound on which there was the site of an ancient settlement. In a subsequent paper, part of which was quoted in his book on the history of Abington Pigotts and Litlington, Rev. Pigotts showed a surprising ignorance of the nature of the bed but described what the diggers had unearthed.

"most of the arable land here was dug for coprolites or petrified fish bone, used for manures. In March 1882 a low eminence (Bellus Hill) was dug. A rectangular enclosure of hollows and ditches revealed an ancient village, with closes, yards and houses, surrounded by a stockade. It was dug to a depth of 20 feet. Four cartloads of artefacts were removed, thought to be Roman."

(Pigott, Rev. G. (1937), 'History of Abington Pigotts and Litlington,' p.32; Kiln, A. op.cit. p.47; PCAS,6,1886 appendix LXIX,30

Early in 1887 Mr. Colchester's workmen had dug the field to the north of Bassingbourn in which the remains of the medieval

Castle, John O' Gaunt's House and its moat, were to be seen. The whole area was turned over and the moats were, to a large extent, filled in. The stones of the moat bridge and other foundation stones were removed and used to mend the roads, no doubt repairing the damage done by cartwheels of the coprolite traffic. (Cambs. Archaeological Record 01776; VCH, vii, 'Cambs.', 2, 1948, pp.15-16) There are no records of any archaeological finds being made by the diggers in the Mordens but that doesn't mean the occasional artefact did not find its way into a digger's pocket.

There is a report that one discovery caused all sorts of excitement in a pit in Hinxworth. Audrey Kiln reported Tom Hedger's story. He was one of the Hinxworth diggers who threw up a pot he had uncovered in a pit which burst open to disclose five hundred well-preserved silver coins bearing raised designs. He told her that in 1876 he

> "had the good fortune to turn up an earthenware vessel containing silver coins all imprinted with seven stars. These he sold, according to Mr. Street, for a handsome profit, which enabled him to become landlord of the then vacant 'Three Horseshoes', a less arduous and far more lucrative occupation."

(Kiln op.cit.p.47)

Whether the coins were bought by a local museum or ended up in private hands is unknown. There were similar accounts of hoards being "discovered" in Shillington and other parishes. It was also 1876 when, according- to archaeological reports, evidence of a Romano-British occupation site (TL255409) was uncovered during the diggings in Ashwell End, north-northwest-of Bluegates Farm. Some small copper coins, (some dating up to the 5th century), a quern and animal bones came to light. Another archaeological find was made in 1882 from coprolite workings just northeast of Bluegates Farm beside Common Lane. It was an Iron Age bone comb used in the weaving process which can now be seen in the Ashmolean Museum in Oxford. (Sheldrick, (1991), p.12; Herts. County Archaeological Record 0415, 4449, 0173; VCH Herts, IV, (1914), p.148; Cussans: History of Herts. 3., p.316, OS Records, Morris: Gazetteer; also see O'Connor, B. 'The Morden Fossil Diggings', Bernard O'Connor, Gamlingay; O'Connor, B. 'The Coprolite Industry in Shillington', Bernard O'Connor, Gamlingay)

During the forty years or so of the coprolite industry entrepreneurs like Herbert Fordham, Swan Wallis, Edward Packard, Henry Coningsby and William and Edward Colchester dominated the work in the area and probably worked over a thousand acres between them. Paying landowners an average £100 an acre it would have amounted to approximately £100,000. Selling the coprolites at an average of £2.50 a ton before labour and capital costs they could have made hundreds of thousands of pounds. Although the numbers employed were not huge, their higher wages would have provided many families with a better standard of living than agricultural labourers. Certainly there were still may poor families at the time but this new industry helped temporarily to slow down out-emigration, cottage industries expanded and diversified and a number of new skills were learned, particularly in the use of machinery.

Farmers and coprolite contractors' business stimulated other trades. Local carpenters gained useful work in the erection and repair coprolite sheds, making coprolite trucks and cutting timer for planks and supports. (Corresp. J. McNeice, Melbourn re. old builder's account books) Blacksmiths would have had work making and repairing tools and shoeing horses. Surveyors, solicitors and auctioneers made good business out of the arrangements between landowners and contractors. Bankers would have profited from the loans made to speculators in the industry. Brewers, shopkeepers and other traders would have benefited from the increased spending power generated by the industry. Carters would have made a good trade taking coprolites to the mills and stations. An iron works was established in Bassingbourn where much of the coprolite plant and machinery was made. Cottages were constructed, new farmhouses and outbuildings were built, new churches and chapels were erected or renovated and much improvement was done during this period.

What was done with the money realised by the diggers is not known. Purchasing land, building houses and renovating property was common but probably a lot would have been spent on food, clothes and drink. The coprolite diggings brought this area a level of prosperity never experienced before or since. (O'Connor, B. (1999), 'The Dinosaurs on Bassingbourn Fen', Bernard O'Connor, Gamlingay)

Table I. The Age distribution of the Mordens' Coprolite Workers - 1861 - 1891

Age Group	1861		1871		1881		1891	
	Guilden Morden	Steeple Morden	Guilden Morden	Steeple Morden	Guilden Morden	Steeple Morden	Guilden Morden	Steeple Morden
11 - 14	0	0	3	1	0	2	0	0
15 - 19	0	0	13	5	11	5	0	0
20 - 24	1	0	17	9	9	9	0	0
25 - 29	0	0	12	17	5	3	0	1
30 - 34	0	0	8	14	10	2	0	2
35 - 39	1	0	15	9	11	6	0	0
Over 40	0	0	13	14	7	4	0	0

Table II. Home Locations of Morden's Coprolite Workers

Steeple Morden	1871	1881	Guilden Morden	1861	1871	1881
Cheyney Street	3	0	High Street	2	18	15
Church Street	13	6	Bucklers Lane	0	0	1
Mill Street	3	0	Church Street	0	25	10
Odsey Way	4	0	Church Lane	0	3	1
Nr.Station	2	0	Trap Road	0	0	1
Gatley End	4	0	Pound Green	0	2	6
Wet Bottom	2	0	Avenell Place	0	0	1
Notts Bridge	8	0	Green Knole Road	0	0	2
The Green	6	2	Little Green	0	10	10
Hay Street	11	4	Great Green	0	11	6
North Brooke End	9	14	Bake House	0	5	0
Bogs Gap	2	1	Fossil Hut	0	1	0
Brooke End	2	1	Dabs Knole	0	6	0
Flecks Lane	0	3